WHO'S WATCHING MY BABY

THE COMPLETE GUIDE TO COMPETENT CHILDCARE

CHRISTINA D. EAGLIN

Ordering Information:
WhosWatchingMyBaby.com

Library of Congress Publication Data is available.

ISBN: 979-8-218-37871-4

Cover design by: Emily Eaglin
Interior design by: Christina D. Eaglin

Published in the United States of America

First Edition Publication Date: Mar 2024
Publisher: MVP Agency LLC

DEDICATION

To Emily and Maya, the two most beautiful people I know, and am blessed to Mother. You both have taught me the unending love and lengths a mother will go through to protect her young. Thank you for weathering the changes in your everyday care from birth through high school. It was a long journey for us all, and you were both fantastic and flexible. Despite bumps along this road, especially when I did not pick the ideal childcare solution, we all survived. I have learned so much from you both and am proud to be your mom and friend to this day.

Love, Mama

Table of Contents

FORWARD

Childcare has a long and sorted history. As far back as the 1800s, those in need of childcare were either immigrants, poor, or minorities. The middle and upper classes could afford the stay-at-home mom, while those who made less were forced to find alternative arrangements for their children. Sonya Michel, PhD at Maryland University, states it best in her article: The History of Childcare in the US;

"Because of its long history and current structure, the American childcare system is divided along class lines, making it difficult for parents to unite and lobby for improved services and increased public funding for childcare for all children. When it comes to public provisions for children and families, the United States compares poorly with other advanced industrial nations such as France, Sweden, and Denmark, which not only offer free or subsidized care to children over three but also provide paid maternity or parental leaves. Unlike the United States, these countries use childcare not as a lever in a harsh mandatory employment policy toward low-income mothers, but as a means of [1] *helping parents of all classes [to] reconcile the demands of work and family life."*

So, now you need childcare, and you're searching for the answers as to what will work best for your family. Where there was once a stigma against parents needing childcare, there is now a high demand for quality childcare. This book was written to enlighten and inspire you and be your go-to when making decisions and working out your childcare plans.

You are not alone; as a single mom, I went through literally every iteration of childcare, which has allowed me to share with you the pros and cons and the pitfalls. Together, we'll dive into my experiences as well as forms and information for interviewing, hiring, and even changing providers when the need arises. I navigated these waters so that you don't have to recreate the wheel as they say.

Very few moms that I've encountered in life have been happy with their childcare arrangements. I repeat, you are not alone! I hope you read, enjoy, and take what you'd like from my experiences. This book is written with a light heart and a firm desire to transform your childcare to an incomparable state of comfort and success.

Every chapter is preceded with a real-life story imparting wisdom, humor and sometimes caution. Brace yourself, though, as my girlfriend says, *"Gurrrrrrl…you won't believe this!"* Some of these experiences may make your blood boil, and others may make your day!

Chapter One: Choices to Make: Stay at home, Work Part time or Full time.

They say the first to know is the mother, and the second is the childcare provider!

Sad but true, most of us cannot afford to be a stay-at-home parent (SAHP) or have the "Super Parent Lifestyle" of baking, cooking, cleaning, and never-ending happiness! So now that your bundle of joy is on the way or here in some cases, you have some critical decisions to make.

To work or not work? Maybe you'll choose to work part-time versus full-time. If you're lucky enough to have a flextime or job-share option, those may also be great solutions. *To take off the legal six weeks of maternity leave only, or to save every sick/vacation day you possibly can to stretch your leave?* Or do you use FMLA (Family Medical Leave Act) if offered at your place of employment? When your leave is over, your daycare adventure begins! Are you prepared? Are you ready?

Should you decide to return to the workforce, full-time or part-time, having your daycare and backup arrangements in place is critical. You will not be as efficient as possible at work if your mind is elsewhere, especially stressing about your beloved child.

The first day I put my firstborn into daycare, I couldn't go to work. I left her at the daycare center in the morning, went home, and bawled my eyes out for the rest of the day. The second day was not much better, but since I was back in the office, my pride wouldn't let me cry in front of the same co-workers who had been carrying my load for four months and, on top of that, were beyond glad to see me return.

The main thing to remember is that your employment decision can change. You may decide to take one option of employment, only to find that another one is better for your parenting style. If you are a single parent, be sure to reach out to your support network to process what might be best for you and your new bundle of joy, as well as any existing bundles that you may already have. If you are married or with a partner, it is critically important that you both agree on childcare arrangements. The last thing you need in a busy two-adult household is drama and "I told you so," which are all preventable through the art of communication. Through the lens of my experiences, the following chapters will aid you in cultivating your very own just right "Goldilocks" childcare arrangement.

Chapter Two: Licensed Daycare Centers (DCC)

STORY: DAISY DAYCARE CENTER

Daisy's is right down the street from our home, so I went in to see about getting my oldest enrolled. They had separate rooms for different age groups and a password-protected entrance, which I liked a lot. They also had a separate house for school-aged kids that their vans picked up from school and deposited at the end of the day.

While in between nannies, I temporarily put the girls in Daisy Daycare. My oldest loved it and made lots of friends. She went on and on about what they did, the things they made, songs they learned and took me through a theater-of-the-mind tour of everything on the playground and what she thought about it.

My youngest was not so impressed when I went to check on her; she was hyperventilating after a long cry on her nap pad with her Tweety Bird doll in hand. The next day I put them in Mariane's care, which was farther away, but my youngest was more comfortable with her.

As my girls got older and were school-aged, I enrolled them again in the after-school program. They were picked up and brought to the playhouse, which was a renovated house for older kids. They both Loved that experience. They got snacks, did homework, and then had their choice of arts and crafts, games, or running around outside on the playground, complete with a large pirate ship and fort!

When you hear or see "911," what thoughts and images come into your head? Close your eyes briefly and think "911" for just 10 seconds. Are you done? Okay. I can bet the image in your head varied significantly from others' pictures. Some may think about a slick sports car, others the phone number for an emergency, while others may have had the tragic memory of one of the most traumatic days in American history.

The point is no two "Daycare Centers" (DCC) are exactly alike. My Daycare center experience can be worlds away from that of a seemingly close friend. Thoughts like this, however, just don't occur to you when you don't have kids. It's once you are thrown into this amazing race of finding affordable, dependable, and safe childcare for your baby that these differences come into play.

When choosing a DCC, knowing the similarities and differences is crucial. Your local government is an excellent source of information for licensed daycare guidelines. A great resource is childcare.gov, where you will find legal adult-to-child ratios, group sizes, and much more. You can also access your state's guidelines at childcareta.acf.hhs.gov/licensing.

According to the U.S. Government, children should have a minimum of 35 square feet of usable play area inside and 75 square feet of outside usable play area space per child.[3] While these guidelines are important, they are just the beginning of your consideration process and not the end-all and be-all for this significant decision. If that were the case, I could just stop writing now and direct you to your local government!

There are other items to look for besides legal regulations for ratios, sanitation, and food preparation. Some of these include the appearance of the other children, staff education levels, and sick policies, just to name a few. You'll be able to observe and inquire about these specifications and others when you tour prospective DCCs and interview their respective directors. I will expand upon the interview process later in the book and what you want to look for when walking through a DCC and talking with the director.

For now, it is perfectly appropriate and welcomed by good DCCs for you to interview them for consideration. Be sure to call beforehand and make an appointment that works for you and the director. They often have standing meetings and reports to do, so you won't want to drop in on them when they cannot give you the time you need. Be clear that you're looking for a DCC and have questions, which should take about 30 minutes or so; this lets them know that you are serious and to block out time for your interview.

Licensed Medical Daycare Centers for Special Needs Children

Medical daycare centers for children play a crucial role in providing specialized care for those with chronic illnesses or medical needs. These centers offer a supportive environment where children can receive medical attention, therapeutic services, and social interaction. This section explores the significance of medical daycare centers in the United States, how parents can access this care, and current locations open for service. Unfortunately, as of this writing, only 20 states offered this type of care for children up to 21 years old, and it is completely up to state funding whether it is implemented or not.

The Importance of Medical Daycare Centers

Medical daycare centers cater to children with a range of medical conditions such as diabetes, asthma, cancer, and developmental disorders. These facilities are equipped with skilled healthcare professionals, including nurses, therapists, and pediatric specialists, ensuring that children receive comprehensive care tailored to their specific needs. The centers aim to improve the quality of life for children and support families by providing a safe and nurturing environment.

Services Offered

1. **Medical Services**: Trained medical staff administer medications, monitor vital signs, and provide treatments as prescribed by healthcare professionals.
2. **Therapeutic Services**: Physical therapy, occupational therapy, and speech therapy are often integrated into the daily activities, promoting the child's overall development.
3. **Educational Support**: Some centers offer educational activities to ensure that children can keep up with their studies while receiving medical care.
4. **Social Interaction**: Interaction with peers facing similar challenges fosters a sense of community and emotional well-being among the children.

Accessing Medical Daycare Centers

Accessing medical daycare centers involves several steps:

1. **Medical Referral**: Typically, a child needs a referral from their primary healthcare provider or specialist to access medical daycare services.
2. **Insurance Coverage**: Check with the child's health insurance provider to understand coverage for medical daycare services. Some plans may cover these services, making them more accessible for families.
3. **Facility Assessment**: Parents should visit potential daycare centers to assess the facilities, meet the staff, and ensure that the center meets the specific needs of their child.
4. **Application Process**: Complete the application process, providing necessary medical records and information about the child's condition.

Current Locations Open for Service

For up-to-date information on open medical daycare centers, parents can contact local healthcare providers, pediatricians, or use online resources. Websites such as the Child Care Aware and National Resource Center for Health and Safety in Child Care and Early Education can provide valuable information on medical daycare centers in specific regions.

Medical daycare centers contribute significantly to the well-being of children with medical needs, offering a holistic approach to healthcare. Accessing these services involves collaboration with healthcare providers, understanding insurance coverage, and evaluating the suitability of individual facilities. By staying informed and engaged, parents can ensure that their children receive the specialized care they require in a supportive and nurturing environment.

Pros of Daycare Centers

- They are regulated by the jurisdiction of their state and county laws.
- Multiple individuals are available to manage emergencies while still maintaining proper monitoring of your child.
    - In the case of a medical daycare center, the staff is licensed and equipped for medical emergencies.
- If one worker falls ill, there are others to take up their slack, so there is always someone available to care for your child.
    - Equally important is that someone who is ill with a communicable condition doesn't feel compelled to work when sick because they are the only caretaker for your child.
- Many are in office buildings and close proximity to where you may work or live making it convenient for drop off and pick up.
    - If the center is near your place of work, you can enjoy lunch with your child and commute together.
- There is great stimulation and socialization in daycare centers, including outdoor playground activities (in most).
- When picking up your child, you can meet other parents and make friends.

- These friendships can be key if you fall ill and need someone to take your child to or from the shared daycare center.
- These friendships can also last a lifetime between your children and yourselves.

- Your primary daycare worker is probably available to moonlight and babysit for you in the evenings or on weekends.
  - This is a great comfort because they know your child and your child is already acclimated to them.
- Importantly, there is likely extensive electronic surveillance equipment in use. This means there are more eyes to deter, detect, and report serious incidents such as visual physical abuse, a child wandering away, and suspicious individuals observing your child in outdoor play areas.

Cons of Daycare Centers

- Germs! A lot of children in close proximity, some of whom are ill and should be at home, is the ideal setting for disease transmission. While good daycare centers will make sanitizing the facility a top priority, nothing will stop an ill child from playing with and infecting your child.
- Packing! You will routinely need to have and transport several changes of clothes, prepared bottles, wipes, diapers, etc., daily to weekly.
  - You will also receive the soiled clothes back and need to wash and redeliver them along with your bundle of joy.

- Getting out of the house with your little one can prove laborious and exhausting before you get to work, even on the sunniest days.

- Inclement weather closings of some daycare centers may not coincide with your office policy. If this is the case, you will need a backup plan. Many centers go by the local school district's inclement weather policies.

- Because of higher child-to-provider ratios, your child may not get the one-on-one attention they would otherwise get in a nanny or in-home daycare situation.

- Any time you put a bunch of kids together, there is sure to be lots of fun, but sometimes other kids (or yours, I hate to say) may be the impetus for starting fights, biting, kicking, or different sorts of uncivilized behaviors. This behavior is more common than not as they are learning to act appropriately; however, it is something to consider.
    - My youngest got bitten in a daycare center, and I about lost my mind. Despite the kind of care you choose, controlling every little thing in your child(ren)'s environment is nearly impossible.

- If you pick up your child late, there will likely be late fees. These fees usually start at $1.00/minute and go up from there.
    - It's always a good idea to have a couple of family or friends on standby if you can't make it to the daycare center on time for pick-up. (See Chapter 17, The Inevitable - Backup Plans for Your Backup Plan)

NANNY AD #1

Happy, exuberant new mom seeks cheerful, professional, quality childcare for a cute baby. Looking for an honest, reliable English speaker with a legal Citizenship status who plays well with kids, reads, writes, swims, drives well, gets along well with adults, and is able to speak up when something bothers them. Additionally, has a good sense of humor, references, and many years of childcare experience a must. Knowledge of nutrition and the ability to serve nutritious meals and snacks. Skilled in arts and crafts; able to construct magnificent works of art out of ordinary popsicle sticks and glue, a plus! Does this sound like you?

If so, we would love to hear from you. Please call the number listed below so we can meet to see if you are the perfect nanny for our loving home.

215-555-1531

Chapter Three: In-home Daycare (IHDC)

STORY: CYNTHIA LICENSED IN-HOME DAYCARE

Cynthia was an older woman with a licensed in-home daycare. Hers seemed to be a perfect arrangement for me since I only had my firstborn, who was a toddler at the time... What I liked most about Cynthia's setup was her learning environment, with lots of interactive alphabet games and educational toys. Her backyard was enclosed with a high fence and literally looked like Disney World! She had every imaginable piece of equipment for the kids to enjoy, from sandboxes to swing sets and seesaws.

However, I did have one particular concern that gave me pause. Cynthia also cared for her disabled husband, who had suffered a stroke. I inquired about her daycare plans in the event that her husband experienced a medical emergency.

She said she had daycare backups and that if needed, her husband would be transported to the hospital by ambulance, and she would join him after backup arrived and the children were covered. I was so impressed with her organizational skills that I decided to give it a try.

Well, the good news is that her husband never had an emergency. The bad news is that I didn't appreciate at the time how many kids Cynthia was caring for. They were more active and older than mine, and with that came bumps, bruises, whooping cough, and unidentified rashes. When this became more the norm, I pulled my daughter out of

Licensed & Unlicensed

In-home daycare (IHDC) is another choice for your consideration. Many of the people who offer this service are themselves moms who choose to work in their homes. When looking into this arrangement, you need to decide whether you want a licensed or unlicensed IHDC solution.

If the IHDC is licensed, then a certificate will be displayed. Be sure to check and confirm that this IHDC has a current and valid license by snapping a quick picture and looking it up online. Also, look online to see if any complaints or reported incidents have occurred. Being licensed means that the IHDC has been checked out thoroughly by the county and meets specific regulations and guidelines that must be strictly adhered to maintain their license. For instance, exit signs must be prominently displayed. There must be two exits, and the designated areas of the home where children are present must be childproofed.

If the IHDC is not licensed, it doesn't necessarily mean it is not a workable solution. I have had a tremendous non-licensed IHDC and an awful one. (See stories about Cynthia and Marian). One of the most important things to recognize is the danger of relying on your instincts and initial feelings when deciding about an IHDC (unless your job is inspecting and licensing IHDCs).

Most of us are not trained to look beyond the obvious indicators of a good versus problematic childcare setting. It takes experience to learn the obvious and subtle indicators of a safe, nurturing learning environment for your child and where to find those indicators. Making wise choices involves blending informed impressions, solid research, in-depth interviews, credible references, and a healthy dose of skepticism (Pro tip: beware of caretakers who try to convince you to overlook something you feel is a serious shortcoming. I once interviewed one who did not use gloves to change diapers. She snapped at me, saying, "Do YOU use gloves when you change your child's diaper? To which I promptly replied, "I only have one child, and I wash my hands before and after changing her. Needless to say, we did not go with her.

Here are some questions you may want to ask yourself when visiting:

1. How did you feel when you entered this home?
2. If you were a kid, would this be fun?
3. Are the play areas sufficient or scant?
4. How many children are being watched here?
5. What are the ages of the children?

a. You don't want to put an infant in with a bunch of curious and active three and four-year-olds. Trust me! I've been there!

6. Are the toys old, new, clean, or soiled?
7. How do the children appear? Sick, healthy, clean, groggy, happy?
8. Can I trust this person?
9. Is this house clean? Look up! Are there cobwebs on ceiling fans?
10. Do they have pets?

a. If so, what kind and how do they keep the pets away from the children?

b. Or do the pets interact with the children? How and when? (Like bunnies, hamsters, etc.)

11. Do they take the children out on walks, drives, or outings by public transportation?

a. If so, are there multi-person strollers?

b. How long are the outings?

c. Where do they go?

12. Do they have anyone other than themselves caring for the children?

13. How do they handle emergencies?

14. How do they discipline children?

After you've observed and decided that this IHDC could work for you, have a follow-up conversation with the caregiver. It may not always be a great idea to do this when they are working because they need to pay attention to the children in their care. Make an appointment after hours to come in and interview them. Alternatively, with advance notice, naptime for the children is a good time to interview the caregiver; this gives them time to arrange their day to have undivided time for you. Here are some of the follow-up questions I have asked:

1. What inspired you to open an IHDC?

2. What happens when you are sick or take a vacation?

    a. Some caregivers have backups, and others don't. If they have backups, be sure you and your child meet them and are comfortable with them.

3. Do your parents still pay for daycare when you are on vacation or sick?

    a. Some IHDCs will require paid vacation and sick time. Paid vacation is not unreasonable as it is their business, and like you, they are seeking quality benefits.

4. Do you play music during the day? When, for how long, and what type of music do you play?

5. Do you have the TV on during the day? If so, what type of shows do you watch?

    a. Trust me, ya don't want your child watching soft porn soap operas or Cops!

6. What is a typical day like here?

7. How do you feed the children?

    a. Does this provider cook for the kids, or do you need to bring your food for them to heat up and serve to your child?

8. If they are also caring for a spouse or their child(ren), you need to know what will happen if there is an emergency with that individual.

9. If there are other family members or friends present in the home during the day, what is the nature and frequency of their interaction with the children (make sure you check publicly available registers to see if anyone living in the home is a registered sex offender)

    Note: The U.S. Department of Justice offers an online tool to check your state for sex ls offenders at NSOPW.gov.

10. How long have you been doing this, and how much longer do you intend to care for children?

    a. The last thing you want is to put your infant into a place that will close in a year unless your child is going to school the following year or you plan to move out of the area.

11. How do you manage the stress of your work when you are having a bad day? Can you describe a particularly stressful day and how you coped?

12. When do you handle household responsibilities like cleaning, organizing, shopping, and laundry?

The answers to these questions will assist you in making the right decision for you and your child. One of my best arrangements was with an unlicensed IHDC, and one of the worst arrangements was as well (see Cynthia's story)!

Pros of In-home Daycare

- Most providers genuinely love childcare and have crafted a business in their homes around their passion, unlike daycare centers, which may employ people doing it only for the money.

- There's more one-on-one involvement with your child; that, of course, depends on the number of children and staff (if any) they have, but generally, there are not more than 3-4 children.

- Usually, IHDCs have an easy drop-off in a residential area; you don't have to deal with traffic and parking.

- If they have their own older children, this could be a fantastic socialization for your child and theirs.

- Most IHDCs cost less than daycare centers since they don't have the high overhead of a commercial setting.

Cons of In-home Daycare

- When your IHDC provider is ill, you will need to have a backup plan if they do not have one. (See Chapter 17, The Inevitable - Backup Plans for Your Backup Plan)

- If your IHDC provider has a family emergency, you will need to be able to make alternative arrangements for your child if they do not provide them.

- If the IHDC is unlicensed, you will need to look out for hazardous objects, signs, or situations if they exist.

    - Again, just because they don't have a license doesn't make them dangerous. I had a great experience with an unlicensed IHDC. After my kids grew up, the provider moved into an official location and now has a thriving licensed daycare center. I smile to think that, in some small way, I helped a woman start her own successful business.

- Rules and regulations tend to be a bit laxer in unlicensed IHDC situations. You will need to be strict about who can and cannot pick up your child.

- Because it is an in-home situation, you'll also need to be clear on the health policy (it is often unlikely that one exists) but be sure to ask how sick kids are handled.

- The bad IHDC experience that I had let any kid in any condition attend the daycare. As a result, my daughter frequently got rashes and colds, and she ended up in the ER with a bad case of whooping cough.

- If the provider has older children or other adults present in the home during the day, these individuals are a potential source of abuse, which the provider may be unaware of or reluctant to report to you or authorities.

    - Family members present in the home could have possible toxic behavioral patterns, which could place your child at risk.

- In settings such as unlicensed homes with a lone caretaker who likely has multiple children in their care, there may be no on-site backup to assist in emergencies.

NANNY AD #2

Optimistic mother seeks excellent childcare for active and adorable toddler. Looking for a reliable, English-speaking person. Must be able to swim, play with children, and have childcare experience as well as legitimate references. Reading, writing, and legal citizenship status preferred. A pleasant, happy, and positive attitude is greatly appreciated. Please call the number listed below.

215-555-1531

Chapter Four: Live-in Nannies

STORY: LIVE-IN NANNY LAUREL

Well, there we were again in need of daycare, and this time I decided to go with a nanny website. Laurel passed my phone and in-person interviews and was ultimately hired. During the interview, she said her car would be out of the shop before she started. Well, that did not happen. I was suddenly put into an extreme backup mode to successfully transport my kids around. This transportation ended up being via my mother, neighbors, and friends.

I began to wonder how much childcare experience Laurel really had, firstly due to this issue of transportation and secondly to ongoing instances of hearing my own child scream. The first time Laurel was brushing her teeth with HOT WATER! And the second time she zipped my child's neck up into her onesie (note: always put your thumb over the top of zippers!). As if that wasn't enough, when I came home from work one day, I didn't see Goldie, our family's prize goldfish of 5 years from the county fair (don't judge, LOL!). I did notice that his bowl was clean, but no Goldie. I asked Laurel, who proudly announced that she took it upon herself to change the water. Well, you cannot put freshwater fish into tap

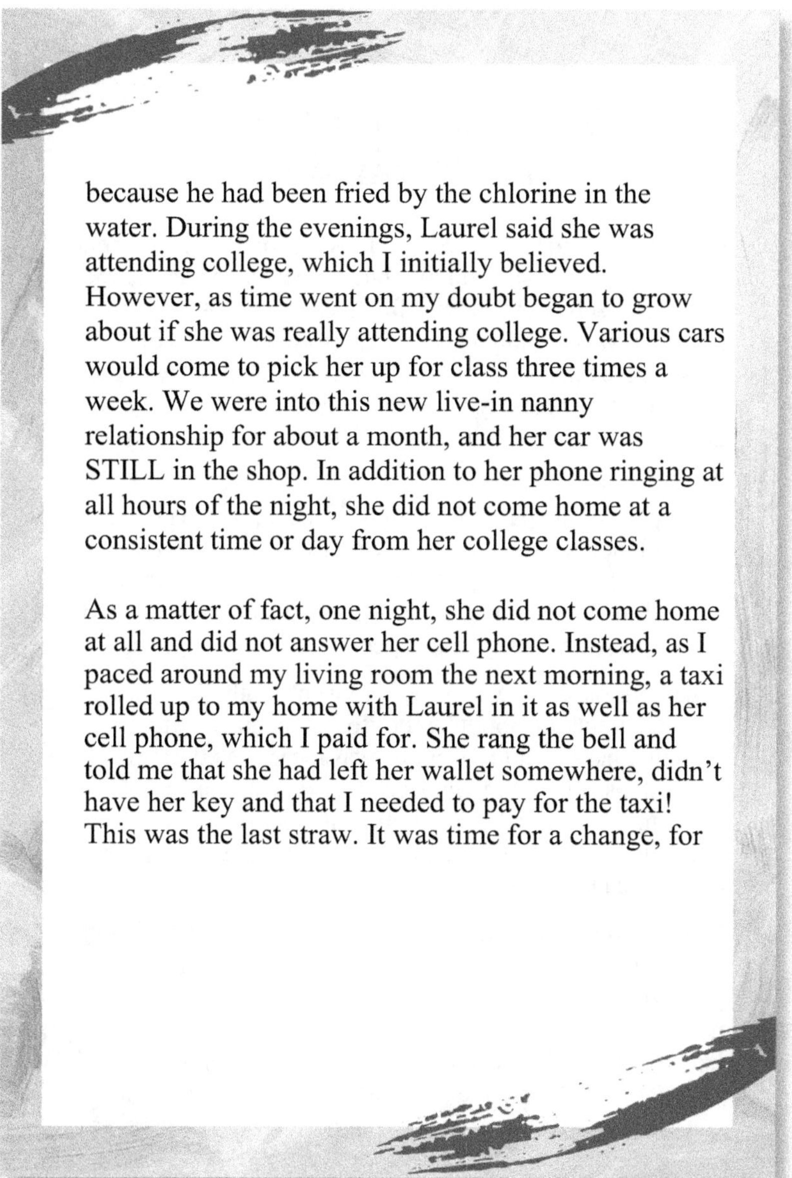

because he had been fried by the chlorine in the water. During the evenings, Laurel said she was attending college, which I initially believed. However, as time went on my doubt began to grow about if she was really attending college. Various cars would come to pick her up for class three times a week. We were into this new live-in nanny relationship for about a month, and her car was STILL in the shop. In addition to her phone ringing at all hours of the night, she did not come home at a consistent time or day from her college classes.

As a matter of fact, one night, she did not come home at all and did not answer her cell phone. Instead, as I paced around my living room the next morning, a taxi rolled up to my home with Laurel in it as well as her cell phone, which I paid for. She rang the bell and told me that she had left her wallet somewhere, didn't have her key and that I needed to pay for the taxi! This was the last straw. It was time for a change, for

STORY: "PROSPECTIVE" LIVE-IN NANNY TATIANA

Okay, so I decided that perhaps looking for a nanny myself may not be the best solution. I hired a nanny agency that claimed to screen its nannies fully. The results were terrific; it was literally like a candy store with loads of prospective nannies to choose from. After I spoke with the prospective nannies by phone and decided they may be a good fit, I would always host the interviews outside my home.

I really liked one particular nanny, Tatiana, on the phone and included her on a playdate with my girls. We went to an indoor playground, and it was a total lovefest! She was warm, kind, and caring; my girls immediately gravitated to her. I was ready to sign the papers!

When our playdate was over, it all went south. Somehow, she started talking about her boyfriend on our way to dropping her off. It turns out he was incarcerated for the use and distribution of crack cocaine, and she had a restraining order on him. Additionally, her phone was police-issued in the event he ever showed up to harm her. (Deep breath here!)

I have never been so disappointed not to hire anyone in my life. The agency was belligerent and asked me what her jailed boyfriend had to do with Tatiana's capabilities as a nanny. While this point may be valid, this position is not like an office job. The mere fact that her boyfriend could get out or send someone to do his bidding was something I

If you are a very private person, cannot stand the thought of someone going through your valuable possessions, or even live with many locked up, password-protected, and guarded idiosyncrasies, then this option is not for you (you might as well stop here and skip the following two chapters).

I once hired a nanny who said there were post-it notes all over the house, she was working in that instructed her not to touch, open, or go near certain items and places in the owner's absence. Naturally, these turned out to be a concise road map to everything the woman didn't want her nanny to know about (and I mean *everything*! Ya gotta love the human spirit). This nanny and a soon-to-be long-time family friend had me laughing so hard at all the things this woman thought her "oh so powerful" Post-it notes would protect her from.

Note to self: Post-it notes do <u>not</u> protect your privacy and are not only a road map to your potential invasion but also a hugely passive-aggressive insult to your nanny!

Okay, enough of the negative already. If you have room (a significant consideration, particularly with live-in nannies), and you're okay with sharing your space, this could be one of the most rewarding and convenient arrangements you can make for yourself and your child(ren).

However, let me give you a word of caution on non-childcare duties. The mental welfare of your nanny is paramount. A happy nanny equals a happy child. If you overload your nanny with too many non-child-related responsibilities, you could overwhelm them and ultimately lose them to another family.

I once had a live-in nanny whose previous family made her wash the family cars and chop wood (no joke!). The worst part was that the family owned a large (and famous) department store and had her on the payroll as an employee. It got so bad that although she loved the children, she was treated like an indentured servant to absentee parents and had to leave the family.

Additionally, I have always believed that non-childcare duties should be done when kids are napping or secured in a visible play area. I never wanted to hear from my nanny: "____ happened when I was cleaning the toilet today." Therefore, I have another woman who comes to do the hardcore cleaning; to me, it's another expense; however, it's worth my peace of mind and gives me more time with my kids when I am not working, which is priceless.

Along with the concerns of the preceding considerations, there are more things to consider with a live-in nanny. Your live-in nanny must have private space and clearly understand their working hours. Additionally, set limits on curfews and exceptions for when it's acceptable for them to be out on weeknights and weekends. If they are using your car, can they use it on their own time? Are you okay with them going on highways or following restricted use privileges? Some families give the vehicle a curfew instead of the nanny to avoid conflict with their car going out at all hours of the night when their nanny is not working. They make it clear that the car is for transporting the children only and not a personal car for the nanny. You'll have to decide for yourself about this and if you want to add the nanny to your insurance policy.

I once had a nanny who would come home between 2 am and 7 am. These grand entrances disturbed the entire house (not to mention the two poodles who lived to alert and protect us with their high-pitched barks in stereo!) These arrivals also disrupted my sleep because I would have thoughts that something awful may have happened to her, which would be bad for both of us. These late hours were always on a work night, which (against the backdrop of her premise of taking college courses and depending on friends and relatives for a ride because her car was "Still in the shop") always left me feeling like a zombie the entire next day. On one occasion, she showed up in a taxi at 7:30 am, and I had to pay the driver because she had lost her wallet. (Of course, the time for me to leave work was 7 am, and now I was a full half hour late).

Telephone and internet use are hot spots to watch out for when you have a live-in or live-out nanny. To avoid surprises on your bill, you should agree that they use phone calling cards if they are on your phone plan, and it is not unlimited. Many of the nannies I had were from other countries, and the internet was their sole source of communication with their family and friends across the ocean. This lovely party girl nanny, with the early morning taxi, left me with a $900.00 bill to 1-800-HOT-DATES. Trust me, as I am a single, hard-working mom, I can assure you I did not make any of those calls! For these reasons and so many more, it is vital to have your expectations both respected and met. Fortunately, nowadays, there are cell phone apps for free hot dates and communication worldwide. If you supply a work phone to your nanny, you want to develop rules regarding apps and "other" charges; include this in your work agreement, which we will get into later in this book.

With live-in nannies, there are also some super sweet rewards. The fact that you can each support and rely on each other can be gratifying. Opening your home and heart to a non-family person teaches your child(ren) to respect and appreciate diversity and to honor and celebrate others' differences on multiple, more intimate levels.

Pros of Live-in Nannies

- They live with you! There is no dressing, packing, loading up bottles, food, and clothes to transport to another daycare solution.

- Your child does not have to disrupt their morning by being moved from the comfort of their home. Especially if and when your child becomes ill, they will be able to stay home with your nanny to recover.

- Learning and sharing different foods, cultures, and customs can enhance not only your family's life but the life of your nanny, too!

- If your nanny speaks a different language, you can have your child learn that language and be fluent in two languages before preschool.

- Guaranteed childcare when you need it the most is always a plus! In situations such as having a late-night meeting, event, or conference to attend, you always know that your nanny is at home and has your back.

- Sometimes, you might leave something, and they can bring it to you or have it couriered. If you forget to do something, they can do it for you, like mailing a stack of envelopes on a table.

- Nannies will meet your neighbors and friends and can also babysit for them, which allows them to make a little extra cash outside of their working hours (with your permission, of course!).

- Taking a nanny on vacation with the family can provide an abundance of freedom for you and your significant other to get away and have some "adult fun!."

- If you work non-traditional hours such as overnights or evenings, this solution is excellent because your nanny will adjust to your schedule when you cannot be home with your kids.

- Nannies can get your child(ren) bathed, put to bed, awoken, and dressed before you even get home, depending on your work schedule.

- If your nanny drives, they can transport your kids to all their activities, do drop-offs and pickups at school, as well as grocery shop for the family; leaving you with more quality time to spend with your child(ren).

Cons of Live-in Nannies

- They live with you! This means you need to be comfortable with them having 100% access to your home and everything under your roof.

- Depending on how many children you have, you may find that they aren't getting as much peer socialization as other children; this is easily rectified with organized play groups.

- If your nanny gets sick, you will most likely be caring for them because your home is their home, and they will need you.

- If your nanny has a significant other, they may be around your children, and you will need to make sure you are comfortable with this, as well as if you want your nanny to have any overnight guests.

- If you provide a car to your nanny, I recommend adding them to your insurance. This could be a significant investment depending on their driving record and age.

    - When your nanny is not working, will they still be able to use the car you provide? Some families put a curfew on the vehicle to avoid it being out all hours of the night.

- While vacations are fun with nannies, they will add to your vacation budget. You should factor in their meals, activities with your child and give them a room of their own unless they are cool with sharing your children's space.

- Unless you work from home, if your baby is pre-verbal, they cannot tell you what happened during their day; you may want to consider a live-in nanny after your child can talk.

    - If there is an older sibling who is verbal, this may work out better for you, as they will be more apt and able to communicate about their day.

NANNY AD #3

I'm looking for childcare. I would prefer to hire someone who actually likes children! I'm looking for someone reliable who shows up on time, speaks English, swims, and can cook. Call the number if this is you. I look forward to hearing from you.

215-555-1531

Chapter Five: Live-out Nannies

STORY: MARIZA LIVE-OUT NANNY

I used to get my hair done at JCPenney's by a guy named Steve. Next to his station worked Mariza, who I would always talk to when I was there. She had five children and was extremely smart and bright. One day, Mariza overheard me speaking with Steve about my concerns that I had to get rid of my nanny Verna. When I left that day, Mariza gave me her number and asked me to call her; she said she had someone she thought could work out for me. I called her later that evening and was thrilled to learn that SHE wanted the position. She said she could work her hours such that she could watch my children for me. We had Mariza for many years, and it was literally like having Mary Poppins come over every weekday. Mariza would do amazing art projects with the girls and hang their works all around the kitchen walls (complete with hand and footprints, of course). She would take them out and record on our camcorder their expeditions to the playgrounds, amusement parks, zoo, and more (this was before cell phones recorded video, of course!). She was an amazing cook, particularly of Peruvian food, and my girls got their hair styled in all kinds of great ways since she was also a licensed beautician. As Mariza's five children aged, she needed to devote more time to them at home and had to leave. That said, she showed up every Easter with handmade baskets for my girls. We attended each of her children's birthday celebrations and her graduation from college. To this day, we love Mariza as if she were family. We are best friends, and her husband just celebrated his 70th, which my girls and I attended.

STORY: LIVE-OUT NANNY LIBBY

We were lucky enough to live in a neighborhood that had its own bar/ restaurant, Andariego's, where neighbors often meet. As a single mom, I was often too tired to cook dinner and would just take my girls out at least once a week. This was a treat for them and a well-needed break for me. They loved to go to Andariego's because the server knew them by name and always gave them special attention. She would make amazing Shirley Temples with a TON of cherries (more than the law would possibly allow), complete with umbrellas and fruit garnishes. Her name was Libby, and she would come and sit down at our table and always speak with us. She would inquire as to what was happening in the girls' lives, and she genuinely cared about them and remembered every detail so she could follow up with them on our next visit.

Libby had always been in the food service industry but had a natural love and energy for kids; she never had kids of her own. When I decided it was time to change nannies, I reached out to Libby to see if she would be interested. She jumped at the opportunity, made more money with us, and enjoyed her work life in our home. As a bonus, Libby was an excellent cook and often included the girls in meal prep. She became my right hand. Libby would meet me with the kids for pediatric appointments, take them wherever needed, and never complain about other kids coming to the house. I believe she loved having as many kids around her in our house to watch as possible.

On several occasions, she invited the girls over to her apartment for a slumber party. When they came home, they would be beaming with all the fun things Libby had done with them. This made them feel so special and gave me a nice FREE break. To this day, we are still friends with

If you are considering a live-out nanny, you must be comfortable with having someone in your home when you are not there. Just like the live-in nanny solution in the previous chapter, you really need to consider whether you or your significant other will be comfortable knowing that there is a person who can pretty much go and do anything in your home without your knowledge. Therefore, if you're still squirming while reading this, consider these facts before committing to live-out nannies.

I have had great live-out nannies. We once had a live-out nanny who was Buddhist. My children enjoyed going to the temple, attending holy ceremonies, eating fantastic food, and dancing to cultural music from Sri Lanka. Another Nanny from South America's custom was to pop over 500 balloons at midnight with plastic forks, dance to great music, and, of course, eat amazing food! I found myself begging to go home at 4 am and dragging my defiant three and 5-year-olds off the dance floor! We loved the learning and sharing of other cultures our nannies brought into our lives, and we are all the better for it.

So basically, if you are an open-minded, free-spirit type, a live-out nanny could work out perfectly for you. Especially if your work requires you to stay late, attend evening events, or you must work evenings, your child(ren) won't be disturbed from the comfort of their own home.

Another thing you may wish to negotiate is your nanny watching other children who may drop by to play with your child. Consider including this in your agreement if it is not frequent. Infrequent visits shouldn't have to cost you. Also, 1-2 nights out per week can be part of your agreement. Of course, you must also work out vacation time and sick leave for your nanny. Whether live-in or live-out, I always give two weeks of paid vacation after six months of employment. In my agreement, I state we both must agree on vacation time so that I can be sure my children are covered when my nanny is not available. Often, these vacation windows would be during my planned vacation so that I could spend significant time with my girls. These are some considerations for having a happy and healthy working relationship with your nanny.

Pros of Live-out Nannies

- They live with you only during the day and go home at night. This arrangement is less invasive than the live-in nanny or au pair because you regain your home again after they leave.

- Your weekends are yours with your family to do as you like.

- You are not obligated to take them on vacation or include them in family functions like the au pair. However, if you want them to come, you can usually arrange that for an additional fee.

- They also have all the pros of a live-in nanny.

Cons of Live-out Nannies

- If they are late, this could disrupt your day.

- If they don't drive, and you must pick them up from the bus stop, this could prove tiresome, not to mention if they miss the bus and you have to go pick them up across town (yup...been there done that one too; there was no Uber when I had childcare).

- If you have an active evening schedule, they may not be available to help given their own family or commitments outside of your household.

- They are the only ones at your house with your child. As mentioned, this solution is ideal for verbal toddlers/children who may or may not have non-verbal siblings.

- Many times, these nannies have their own children and lives, and you will need strong backups when they need to tend to their family illnesses or emergencies

- Additionally, live-out nannies also have all the cons of live-in nannies.

NANNY AD #4

I'm a super exhausted mom looking for someone to care for my child. I need someone reliable, on time, and English speaking.

215-555-1531

Chapter Six: Au Pair

STORY: AU PAIR CARLA

I decided to try an Au Pair agency based on the fact that my dear friend Belinda had such great success with this agency. Her Au Pair was with her children for years and truly was part of their family. She put me in touch with the folks who had placed her au pair in her home, and I just "knew" I was on my way to victory! The problem was that there were no au pairs available at the time I was looking. And then it happened.... Belinda called me to tell me that her au pair knew of another one who was unhappy with the family and wanted to be placed in another home because the family was too strict and she was very uncomfortable.

We made arrangements for me to meet with this young lady, and my kids and I thought she was terrific and had just hit a bad family, which does happen. We approached the agency and Carla checked off my requirements of swimming, cooking, driving, and genuinely loving to care for kids.

So, the big day arrived, and we went to pick Carla up to join our family. The first stop was my mom's of course so she could welcome her into the family. The girls and Carla jumped in their bathing suits and hit Mom's pool. As I was in the kitchen with my mom she looked out the window saying, "I thought Carla could swim?." She can I exuberantly replied. Then she told me to look out the kitchen window, and to my shock MY GIRLS were TEACHING her how to

After we finished our visit, I told Carla to drive us home since my mom only lived 1.5 miles away. Carla proceeded to drive my van into the side of my mom's low wooden retaining wall. When we got to the main road, she didn't do much better. When we finally did make it to our home, which seemed like an eternity, she damn near ran

into my house while attempting to park. Her excuse was that she is used to driving a stick shift and the automatic transmission was more difficult; yeah right. Mind you she has a VERIFIED INTERNATIONAL DRIVING LICENSE!!! [Strike Two]

Because I had invested so much money with the agency, I decided to get Carla driving lessons from a bi-lingual teacher because her English was not as proficient as her papers indicated. After her first class, the teacher came back screaming at ME! She said, "This woman cannot drive, she has never driven, she will kill you, she will kill your children, she will kill people in the street and she damn near killed me!" [Strike Three].

I could overlook the green chicken she boiled with broccoli, the fact she appeared to only eat marshmallows, and the late-night internet calls in my office adjacent to my bedroom to speak with her relatives in Venezuela. But what I could not overlook was that she was completely unqualified for the job.

I let her know that I was going to have to let her go and she almost looked relieved. She then told me that she would be leaving on her own and attempting to claim asylum in the States because she did not want to go back to her country. So, she said goodbye to us all and we wished her well as she disappeared into the country.

Pronounced <Oh-Pear>, an au pair is another solution to your childcare needs. The term comes from the French, meaning "on par" or "an equal". These infant and childcare providers are from foreign countries, ranging from late teens to mid-twenties. There are many agencies and websites offering placements for au pairs. Each agency has its way of screening its au pairs. Some au pairs will take college classes around your schedule as a requirement, while others will not.

The most significant difference is that an au pair is expected to be a part of your family instead of an employee. They can still have the same responsibilities as a nanny, but you are expected to include them in meals, family outings, and vacations. This can be a wonderful experience for a home with a lot of room and an open-minded family. Au Pairs generally cost significantly less than a nanny because you include them in your family and provide them food and shelter, and they do not have another home they need to support.

If they don't work out, there are immediate replacement options from the agency or website you found them on (please don't ask me how I know, lol!). However, when they do work out, they can stay with you for many years and help to make your childcare needs a beautiful experience.

- They are like having an older child who is very helpful around the house and makes life easier for your family.

- The exchange of cultural celebrations, foods, and customs can be exciting for everyone.

- If they speak a different language, it is an excellent opportunity for your child(ren) to learn a second language.

- The placement agency can provide direction and a replacement if the au pair doesn't work out.

- They also have the same pros as live-in and live-out nannies.

Cons of an Au Pair

- They live in your home, and if you're not comfy with it, you may not want this solution for your child(ren)

- While they are less expensive than a nanny or daycare center, there is an agency fee. Depending on which agency you select, this fee could be steep, plus you typically will pay for their visa and transportation to the States.

- If they are looking to defect from their country, you could lose them. I had one with a similar situation that was a bit different (see Carla), and she told me she was going to run away and that I should make other arrangements because she couldn't return to her country. She checked in occasionally, but honestly, I was going to replace her anyway, so this worked out for both of us!

- There could be a language barrier if they aren't fluent in English. Many barely speak English; however, the au pairs I have known learned quickly.

- Be wary of their skill sets. I was told Carla could swim, drive, and speak fluent English. None of these things were true! I have no idea how the hell she scored an international driver's license. When I bought driving lessons for her (very expensive and out of my desperation), the instructor literally came back after driving with her and screamed at me, yelling that Carla had NO experience and would kill my kids, me, and people on the street. (Yeeeesh!)

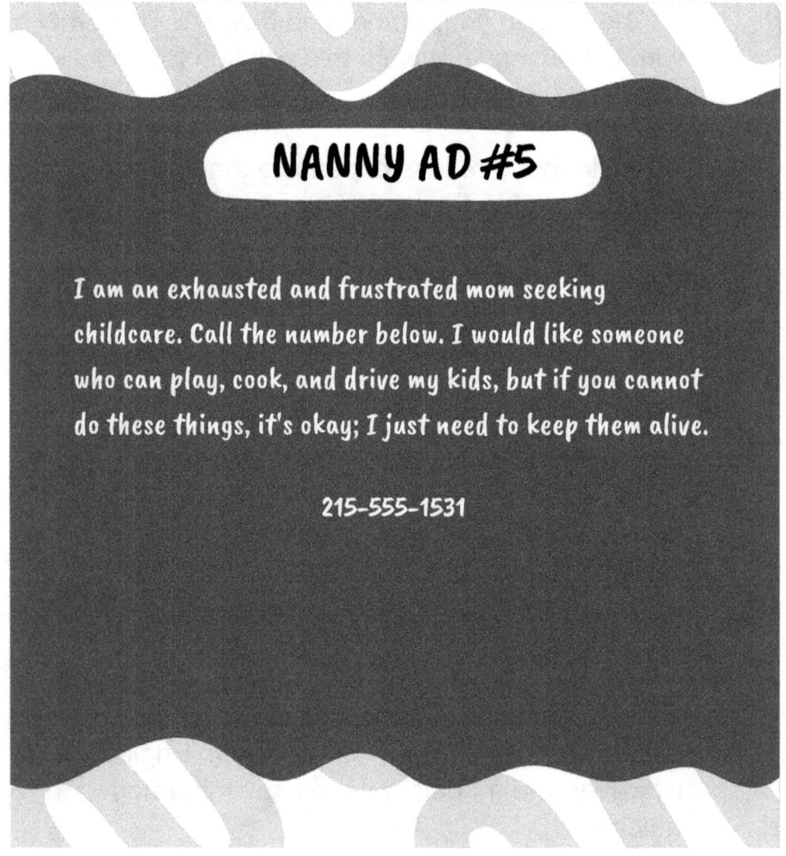

NANNY AD #5
I am an exhausted and frustrated mom seeking childcare. Call the number below. I would like someone who can play, cook, and drive my kids, but if you cannot do these things, it's okay; I just need to keep them alive.
215-555-1531

Chapter Seven: Nanny Sharing

STORY: LIVE-OUT NANNY VERNA & HER SON

When I needed daycare for my second child, I crunched the numbers and determined having a live-out nanny would be more economical. I was very pleased with my current daycare center provider, Verna, and successfully hired her away from the center. What I wasn't aware of was how many interfering priorities she had.

Her son came to work with her because of the distance they lived away from my home. I enrolled him in our neighborhood elementary school. What started smoothly quickly became broken toys and spats between her son and my daughter. Because my oldest was exceptionally verbal (which is what I highly suggest for this arrangement), she gave me the blow-by-blow of who, what, where, when, and how each toy met its ultimate demise.

Verna also lived in public housing and had to take a bus to work; there were many times when she would be late. Sometimes, she would miss the bus, and I would have to pick her up at her place 30 minutes away (mind you, this was pre-Uber and Lyft). Other times, I would have to pack my kids up and drive to the bus stop. If she caught a late bus, she couldn't walk to my house in time for me to get to work. I also had to drive her to the bus stop to go home. Still, I was optimistic and figured at least I had a person in

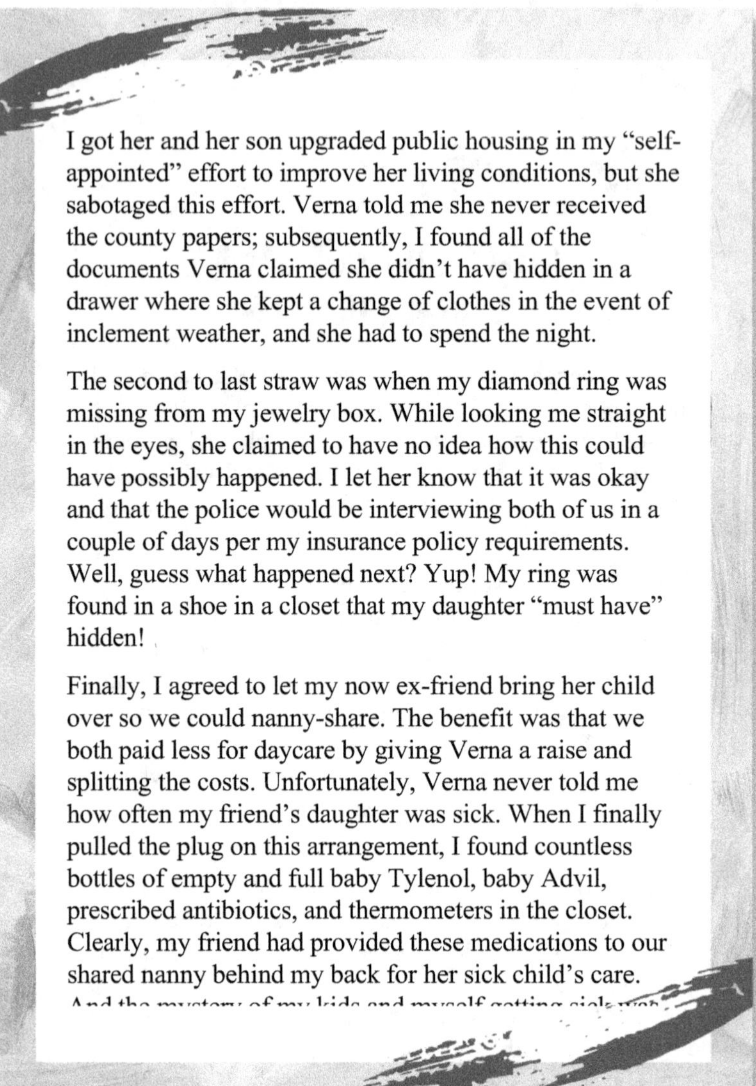

I got her and her son upgraded public housing in my "self-appointed" effort to improve her living conditions, but she sabotaged this effort. Verna told me she never received the county papers; subsequently, I found all of the documents Verna claimed she didn't have hidden in a drawer where she kept a change of clothes in the event of inclement weather, and she had to spend the night.

The second to last straw was when my diamond ring was missing from my jewelry box. While looking me straight in the eyes, she claimed to have no idea how this could have possibly happened. I let her know that it was okay and that the police would be interviewing both of us in a couple of days per my insurance policy requirements. Well, guess what happened next? Yup! My ring was found in a shoe in a closet that my daughter "must have" hidden!

Finally, I agreed to let my now ex-friend bring her child over so we could nanny-share. The benefit was that we both paid less for daycare by giving Verna a raise and splitting the costs. Unfortunately, Verna never told me how often my friend's daughter was sick. When I finally pulled the plug on this arrangement, I found countless bottles of empty and full baby Tylenol, baby Advil, prescribed antibiotics, and thermometers in the closet. Clearly, my friend had provided these medications to our shared nanny behind my back for her sick child's care.

Unlike live-in and live-out nannies, this solution involves multiple families and typically multiple homes. Basically, the nanny is a live-out nanny who rotates between homes. Many families find this more economical because nanny sharing generally costs less since you are both paying the same person to watch your children. Much like the live-in and live-out nanny concerns, you'll need to be sure you are comfortable not only with the nanny coming into your home but also with other children coming into your home. Conversely, you will need to be comfortable taking your child(ren) to the other family's homes when it is the other family's week for the nanny to come to them.

I believed myself to be doing a friend "a favor" and found myself in a nanny-share situation. We lived about five minutes apart, so it wasn't a hardship for us to bring our kids to each other's home every other week. The issue I had was that my friend had an older child living in her home who, I was unaware at the time, was chronically and contagiously sick. My children rarely got ill, and suddenly, we had colds, viruses, and other issues in our home. It didn't hit me until the nanny share ended, and I cleaned out the closet where the nanny kept my friend's child's belongings. I never saw so much Tylenol, thermometers, antibiotic prescriptions, etc. I was furious that the nanny didn't disclose the truth about my friend knowingly bringing over a contagious, sick child with a fever into my home and infecting my entire household.

So, my advice on nanny sharing is to be very careful. It can stress out a relationship if the families aren't clear on expectations upfront. The nanny should never be in a position to have to hide the fact that one of the families is subjecting the other to contagious illnesses; that is not fair to the nanny. If, however, you have strong friendships (mine obviously was not strong enough), and you feel you could cut expenses while having the benefits of a live-out nanny, then sharing a nanny may be ideal for you and your child(ren).

Pros of Nanny Sharing

- Expenses are significantly lower than other solutions since you are splitting them with another family or families.

- Your child(ren) gets socialization with other children.

- You get the benefit of a live-out nanny when it is your week to have the children in your home.

- If shared with friends, you can always rely on friends if you're running late to watch your child for you if the nanny cannot stay late.

- If the nanny drives, they can still do drop-offs/ pickups and get your child(ren) to activities and, in some cases, the other family's home.

- If the nanny is unavailable due to an emergency, sickness, or vacation, you can agree to rotate between the houses who will take off from work and watch the children.

Cons of Nanny Sharing

- When it's not your time to have the children at your home, you will need to pack your little one(s) in all sorts of weather and transport them to the other home.

- If the other children are chronically ill, you can expect to have your child(ren) (and yourself) get ill, too.

- If the nanny is not available, and the other family is unable to watch your child, you will need to have a backup plan (See Chapter 17, Backup Plans for Your Backup Plan)

- The nanny will have multiple bosses, and communication could be impacted. Be sure to have written agreements around expectations of this nanny, who has the final say, and how and when she is paid

- If your friendship breaks down for whatever reason, this solution will most likely follow suit, and you'll need a backup plan.

NANNY AD #6

Are you able to keep a job and like to watch kids? This is not brain science, people! If so, call me. I really need someone to watch this kid so I can go to work!

215-555-1531

Chapter Eight: Stay-at-Home Parents (SAHP) and Part-Time/Job Sharing

This chapter outlines the pros and cons of staying at home and providing your own childcare versus partial in-home care. Obviously, this is a great choice; however, as with the other childcare options, it has pros and cons. Again, I am here to share my knowledge, not to choose your solution or attempt to steer you into any career or life choice that may or may not be suitable for you and your unique situation.

Not everyone can stay at home, but this is a viable choice for childcare if you can, even if it's just for a few days of the week. SAHPs often take a lot of heat from their working peers and friends. The truth is, being an SAHP, in many ways, is harder than being in a demanding job because it's 24/7, and you don't get time off. That said, it's critical to avoid becoming isolated and taking time off when you can (and when you need it).

Many places offer "drop-in" daycare. You'll want to read chapters two and three on licensed and unlicensed daycare centers to figure out if this is possible for the ones in your community. Additionally, there are playgroups, storytelling hours at many bookstores/ community centers, and a plethora of meetups, as well as online parental groups that do things together. Our area has a movie theater that shows movies during the day where babies or toddlers are welcome to scream, roam, and run around in the theater.

Finally, you could still have a nanny who would work alongside you or just on certain days of the week, particularly if you work from home or run your own home-based business and want to have your child(ren) near you with proper supervision.

Work/life balance is just as crucial for SAHPs. The key to being a SAHP is to be organized and have your support system in place, especially if you get sick and are unable to take care of your child(ren).

I became a SAHP when I was laid off from my job. I cried harder about losing my live-out nanny than I did about losing my employment. Paty was excellent and a huge part of our family; we both hugged and cried together as I had to let her go. Today, she has graduated college, married the love of her life (and, of course, we were there for their wedding!), and now has two beautiful babies! One challenge, I believe, is that we aren't adequately educated to be a SAHP. We kind of find our way working through challenges and speaking with relatives and friends for advice. What's nice to know now is that there are free and paid online courses that can assist you in transitioning to being a SAHP, no matter your child's age (see Appendix).

Pros of Stay-at-Home Parenting

- You get to be with your child(ren) daily and watch them develop (first tooth, steps, etc.).
- You don't depend on anyone else to raise your child; you can do it just as you want.
- Your presence becomes even more important once your child(ren) goes to school and begins to establish their circle of friends.

- You don't have to commute anywhere or pack up your child(ren) early in the morning.

- You don't have to rush to the daycare center at the end of the day to avoid late fees.

- Sometimes, with multiple children, it can be cost-effective to stay at home if the daycare center expenses come close to your take-home pay. After all, you don't want to work just to pay your childcare expenses.

- With a good dose of discipline and organization, you can oversee your home (kids, bills, cleaning, shopping, etc.).

- You can always find ways to work from home if you'd like. According to crowdworknews.com, there are great online jobs for stay-at-home parents. https://crowdworknews.com/online-stay-at-home-jobs/

- Since COVID-19 many more work-from-home jobs have emerged.

Cons of Stay-at-Home Parenting

- While being with your child(ren) is rewarding, it can also be isolating and a source of sadness and depression.[5]

- You can be negatively judged by your peers and sometimes be made to feel guilty for staying at home (personally, anytime someone tells me they are an SAHP, I congratulate them and let them know that I know how challenging that is as well as that they work harder than most jobs!)

- Being around children all day can limit your time with adults and make you crave adult time and conversation.

- The routine of staying at home can lead to boredom, so taking advantage of previously mentioned activities and discovering new ones you can share with your child is essential.

- Time management can be challenging with children, household responsibilities, and shopping.

- When you get sick, you won't be able to take care of your child(ren), and because we live in such a transient society, you may be away from your family and friends who may otherwise be near to help out if needed (See Chapter 17, Backup Plans for Your Backup Plan).

- If you choose to work from home, you'll need to be flexible to attend to your child(ren)'s needs.

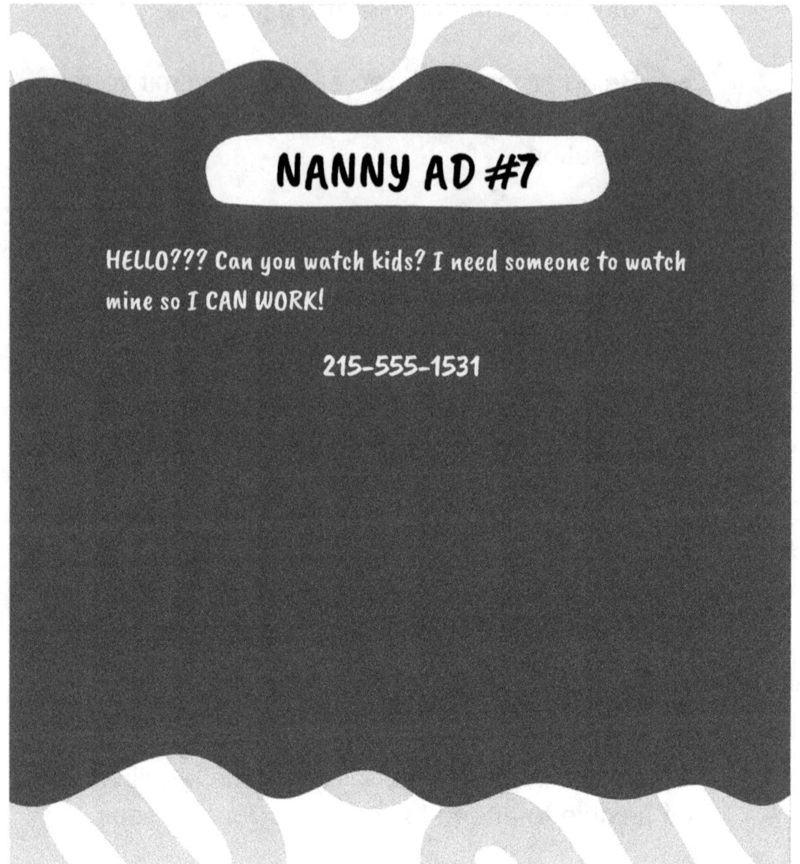
NANNY AD #7
HELLO??? Can you watch kids? I need someone to watch mine so I CAN WORK!
215-555-1531

Chapter Nine: After You've Chosen Your Childcare Solution!

Congratulations! You've decided which solution works best for you and your family. Consider yourself at first base with a home run in mind! If your child is verbal, include them in the process and interviews; after all, they'll be spending the most time with this person. Case in point: I regret not listening to my child for a live-out nanny I once hired out of desperation (note to self and you: do NOT choose a daycare solution out of desperation; it never turns out well!). The following are some additional words of wisdom and red flags for each daycare arrangement.

Daycare Centers

Prepare yourself to be stressed out and depressed the first day (I didn't go to work until the second day). Returning to work is hard enough, but dropping your precious baby off is much harder, trust me. Go easy on yourself and schedule something special for yourself this day. Depending on your baby's age, this may phase or not phase them. Either way, don't allow yourself to be too concerned either way. A crying baby doesn't mean you're a terrible parent. And conversely, a baby who is just fine with this new arrangement doesn't mean you're a terrible parent.

If you can "pop in" to the center unannounced (and I wouldn't pick a center where you couldn't do this), this would be advisable. It is crucial to see how your baby thrives, not just on the first day but throughout their daycare center experience. It may be better for the center and baby if you stay out of sight (if possible) of your child(ren). If you have a "drama mama" like I did, your baby will perform at the mere sight of you, and not always in a subtle way! And last, but not least, be sure to visually check out the health of the other babies in the center as well. I popped in on my daughter at a center once to find a little boy with yellow mucus streaming down his face and no one attending to him. Today, some daycare centers actually have a parent portal where you can see a live stream of your child in their room, get essential announcements, and communicate directly with staff.

It's just as important for you to get along with the staff as they are the ones taking care of your child(ren). It's always a good idea to acknowledge the hard work the daycare center providers give to all their children. Every once in a while, you may consider dropping off a treat for them, like some donuts or candy, to show your appreciation, not just on holidays, of course! A yummy bag of donuts or bagels and cream cheese can go a long way in fostering positive relationships (and you might even get a pass on that late fee once in a while when you get stuck in traffic and can't help being late!).

It may take a while for some babies to adjust, so you'll want to give your center every opportunity over the first week or two. However! If your baby consistently freaks out after the first few days when you drop them off, and they are visibly unhappy when you pick them up, you need to take notice. Also, if your child develops a diaper rash, it could indicate they aren't being changed regularly. Be sure to insist each diaper change is noted and the results thereof (#1 or #2 or both). Most quality daycare centers do this along with keeping a cute "My Day" journal, which tells you what they did, ate, and how they felt as well. These journals are an excellent resource to you and let you know if baby is on track or if there may be some issues that need attention.

Licensed or Unlicensed In-home Daycare Centers (IHDC)

Generally, there are fewer workers in this arrangement. It's usually a woman and maybe an assistant. Therefore, her time is generally taken, and she won't have the flexibility to speak with you as much during her hours of operation. That being the case, you should still do your "pop-ins" and observations as outlined above in Daycare Centers. It's critical for your baby to be a happy customer for you to be a happy employee in your place of employment.

Since the IHDC setup is less formal, see if the provider will let you hang out for a few hours. My non-drama mama toddler daughter and I did this when I moved her into this arrangement, which made for a smoother transition. Again, a happy baby equals a happy parent! Most importantly, don't let your "parental guilt" get the best of you. We must let them go to grow!

Live-in /Live-out Nannies & Au Pairs

Take your time with this solution. The person you hire is in your home with access to your property. If no candidates present themselves immediately, consider a daycare center during your interview process if you need to get back to work. Refrain from being so desperate (as I was) to select the best of the worst.

Once you have chosen a childcare provider, ground rules and a written work agreement (found in the Appendix) are the keys to your survival for this arrangement. Trust me! I "popped in" with a nanny wearing MY workout clothes on my treadmill while my baby was napping! My verbal child at the time was at school. Personally, I do not recommend preverbal infants for this daycare solution unless you have stellar recommendations (be careful, too; other nannies will front as parents of a child who has been in the care of the nanny you are considering). It wasn't until I had my second child that I elected to go for the nanny solution.

Chapter Ten: From the Nanny's Perspective

Nanny Interviews

I conducted three interviews with experienced nannies of differing backgrounds, ages, and ethnicities. One started in her 20s because she knew she didn't want to have a 9-5 job. Another was exhausted with her restaurant waitress job in her 40s, and her customer asked her to care for her school-aged children. The third, now in her 60s, came to the States as an au pair turned nanny. She took advantage of the educational system and got her accreditation in cosmetology and a degree in accounting. She is now a nanny for her grandchildren, still does hair, and has an in-home accounting business.

Why do nannies do what they do?

It all comes down to the love of the children. Resoundingly, each nanny told stories of love about the children they cared/care for every day. They stated that they have a lot of love to give and that sometimes kids need more than love, especially if there is trauma in the home, such as a death or divorce. "When you're working 40+ hours a week, you become everything to that child in their parent's absence," professed one nanny. Another had a love of working with children with special needs such as Autism and Down Syndrome. They genuinely love watching kids develop, nurturing them, and helping the overall family unit.

What has changed the most since you became a nanny?

The following answers to this question were so good I decided to share them directly with you rather than summarize them.

Nanny One: Technology

I think that technology has contributed a lot to change. You can't stop it, and the kids are involved with it, so I must grow and be involved with them as well. In many areas, it is good because you can use technology in many ways. When the kids overuse technology, it is not good. Like too much information that is not appropriate for their age. The children need limits and control.

Food

Parents need to ensure the children eat well. I ask them to provide me with fresh fruit, vegetables, and food for their children. I don't like it when I am asked to give leftover Chinese food, microwaved, or fast food to the children. The microwave destroys the nutrients and flavor, and it doesn't take that much more time to do it the old-fashioned way by using the stove and oven.

Water & Homemade Juices

Water and Homemade juices are very healthy and refreshing. And, from my county in Peru, I make Chicha Morada which is a delicious nutritional juice made from purple corn; it is boiled over two hours, but it is worth it. The color and taste are delicious, and the health benefits are huge.

Nanny Two: Technology

On the one hand, I'm thrilled with the advances in technology that make it easier to do background checks and ensure the kids are safe in their homes with nannies. On the other hand, proper vetting and excellent references, along with continued examples of trustworthiness, are just as vital now, if not more.

Kids today want to spend more time hanging out with their friends in different houses due to technology; they call this a "hang out." They network themselves via electronic games. When kids are younger, they put more focus on creative play, but when they get older, it gets very enticing to play with electronics.

For some kids, it becomes an unhealthy obsession and consumes their lives if not controlled. With the continuation of the changing family dynamic, we are now sitting down with our devices in lieu of our family members. This behavior lessens interactions and socialization, which was once had in the past. It's not uncommon anymore for a person to text another person in the same house instead of just getting up and talking to each other.

Times are different now. Gone are the days of kids coming over and making extravagant forts, arts and crafts, dancing, writing, and performing plays. It's interesting as I reflect back to washing my client's hair. If she would have had electronics, then she couldn't have used them as they would have posed an electrical hazard. This was a special time that forced us to chat and catch up on things. Certain rituals aren't being used as much as they were in the past. My daughter gets her French braid lessons from YouTube now and no longer needs me to do it for her. We've lost some things with technology clearly. This is sad.

Additional Thoughts

There appears to be a lot more respect for the work/life balance and less of a stigma for working moms who have someone watching their kids. Same-sex parents and dads choosing to stay home and let mom be the breadwinner are just some examples of how kids are now viewing their caretakers. It really boils down to the fact that kids just want someone to care for them and to feel safe. They [kids] just want to have a happy and well-balanced upbringing, which is a result of a strong partnership with the nanny and their parents.

Nanny Three:

The economy continues to struggle, and people are looking to make their monthly bill obligations with maybe a little bit of money saved. With daycares charging $300-$400+ per week, it is more economical to have a nanny in your home. A nanny can save you the struggle of loading and unloading kids in the morning and after work. Additionally, your kids get individualized attention, and the nanny can also help you out around your house.

What do nannies really want?

Live-out Nannies Acknowledgement

Professional nannies truly want to feel they are valued members of your family. They want to be positively acknowledged for what they do for you, your children, and your household. They'd like to be trusted and receive perks like surprise bonuses, holiday gifts, oil changes, or gas money when driving their cars.

Respect

Mutual respect is vital to them, and understand that for the nanny, the kids are their priority before any other part of the job. They don't want to be taken advantage of and prefer to stay with one family long-term, even after the children attend school. Live-out nannies most enjoy the children's love and trust in them to provide a safe, fun, and nurturing environment. One of the interviewed nannies put it best, "Children are innocent and need our protection, so it's important to know and trust whoever is taking care of your child."

Accommodation

Making accommodations is also a theme that arose during my interviews. When nannies have their own illnesses or emergencies, it's imperative that the family have a backup plan. Conversely, the parent may get stuck in an after-hours meeting and need the nanny to stay and watch the kids; that accommodation and consideration goes both ways.

Live-in Nannies Boundaries

Boundaries are a more sensitive subject because they don't have their own place to live. They feel it's important to set days and schedules when you will need them so they can plan around their work hours. These situations always require discussion and communication to ensure a mindset where everyone is allowed their own space.

A lot of times, if your child *really* loves their nanny, the child(ren) will want to spend all their time with the nanny. Parents need to realize that their nanny needs a break, and they need to parent when they are home and outside of their nanny's work schedule. The nanny is not a live-in playmate and needs to have their time respected. They need to be able to depend on time off for their own work/life balance.

Transportation

Live-in Nannies typically receive a vehicle for transporting their children and personal use. It's important to have ground rules around the car and its usage. Especially rules regarding texting, seat belt usage, child seats, and speeding, to name a few. You minimize conflict and sore feelings by putting the curfew on the car instead of the nanny.

Cleaning

There is usually some type of housework like light cleaning of the children's rooms, laundry, cooking, or groceries that you may want assistance with from your nanny. It's essential that the nanny is treated as a helper and not as a housekeeper. They will straighten up but not organize or do deep cleaning unless that is negotiated and stated in their work agreement on the front end or you pay them extra.

Socializing

Nannies deserve to have a personal life. However, they should not use it as an excuse to neglect agreed-upon responsibilities. For instance, if your nanny wants to go out on a Thursday to a concert with friends (a day you have asked for laundry to be done), be open to negotiating another laundry day for that week so they can enjoy their personal life just like you do.

Personality Styles

Parents and their parenting styles are very important to match with their nanny. If you act as an overprotective parent (sunblock, bug spray, shoes on, etc.) before they leave the house, you're going to have a lot of frustration with a nanny who sees a cluster of butterflies in your yard and impulsively grabs your child(ren) to go outside and check them out in their bare feet. Some parents are okay with the nanny taking kids out for ice cream; others want to know every bite of food their kid takes, how much food they have, and where their kids go every minute. Be sure your style matches your nanny's style to avoid frustration for both of you.

Huge mistakes we make with nannies.

Nanny One:

"I don't want poor communication; I need to be able to speak to them [about] whatever is going on so that I can deal psychologically with the baby. If something is happening in the family, I need to know what it is. For example, if the baby is not eating or angry, I need to know; I cannot "assume" to know what is going on in their home. I am part of the family in the moment the parents leave, and it is one hundred percent my responsibility to be able to comfort and know the baby. Babies also suffer with depression, particularly when there is tension in the home.

Sometimes, when the parents have asked me to work on potty training or stop a pacifier [habit] that causes problems, we need to have an agreement about how to deal with the kids. My work is every day with their child, except weekends. If the parents don't adhere to our agreement and put diapers on the child or give them their pacifier when I am not in the home, they ruin the efforts that I am working on for their child during the week.

In my experience, I have always had the respect of the children I have watched. Some of the children have gone through their parents' divorcing, and I have had to work with them and their behavioral changes. You have to really be focused to have a really good relationship with the children, as well as the parents."

Nanny Two:

"Sometimes 'assuming' that me staying later is okay without confirming or communicating with me in advance. Or just flat out being chronically late. Sometimes, there can be feelings of not being appreciated or taken advantage of when these things happen.

I haven't really had a lot of mistakes or bad experiences. I've been really blessed to have some really nice families; there was only one that was bat-shit crazy. This woman made me take off my shoes when I came to the house, put my purse on the highest shelf in closet, wash and dry my hands with antibacterial soap, sit down next to her, and read to her 2.5-year-old toddler while she breastfed him every time I arrived. The woman had a minute-by-minute schedule and routine, including clothes, hats, gloves, mittens, boots, and sunblock for our mandatory three-hour stroller walk.

It was ridiculous; she made me sterilize all of his toys weekly and did not allow TV or any type of electronics. He was not allowed any sugar, or soda or processed foods. It turned into a short job (with a quick resignation) when I met the nanny down the street during one of my three-hour walks. The neighbor's nanny told me that the person I replaced used to drive the boy to downtown Washington, DC, and feed him Popeyes Chicken while she talked to her boyfriend. She told the lady she took public transportation and hid her car a few blocks away. Instead of walking, she basically took him away during those three-hour strolls!"

Nanny Three:

"Sometimes they [the family] expect a little too much out of the nanny. They expect you to do things you shouldn't have to do, like spend your own money on the transportation for their kids with your own car. Once, I had to run my air conditioner for half an hour in my car when I went to pick up the kids I was working with; that took up a lot of my gas, which was never repaid or discussed during my hiring.

I want the family I am working for to respect my three-hour minimum, even if I work only for one hour. It is not worth my time or gas to get paid for one hour of time. I don't like to feel like I am being taken advantage of by the family.

Being stingy and treating me like an employee instead of someone who is entrusting me with their children who are with me all day long.

Being too picky or micromanaging me. I actually had to measure the oil for a huge salad and not exceed one tablespoon of oil. The mother said one of her kids only eats foods that are beige, such as hummus, chickpeas, peanuts, pasta, French fries, and more. While I did as directed, I could not help but think that this is the worst nutrition for a kid ever...yuck."

Note: There is indeed a diet called the Beige Diet, and it is not healthy for children. This type of diet will not provide the vital nutrients a growing child's body needs. For more information on the Beige Diet, check out the Bay State Parent's article: Is Your Child on the BEIGE DIET, by Kate Scarlata, RD, L DN[6].

Is There Anything Else You Want to Add?

Nanny One:

With the babies, it is so important to play with them often. I love to rock and sing and laugh with them and play fun bouncing lap games. Even though sometimes the moms don't like it when I tell them about the foods they are giving to their children, I still speak up to let them know the effect that food has on the child. You can make food fun, like Mickey Mouse pancakes, and involving the children in the preparation of their meal. You have to be creative with kids to keep their attention. You have to be smart about watching the kids trying to hide foods they don't like. I had a little girl who would put food under her placemat; I then removed the mat. Then, the same child started putting the food up her sleeves; I made sure she wore a T-shirt when I fed her. She was too smart! I took this same child out to the mall, and she had to go to the bathroom when she was three years old. I asked her if she was sure she had to go, and she proudly said, "I need to go poopy...do pee pee...and pass gas!"

It is so beautiful to give love and receive love back from the children you watch. When they grow up and become adults, it is an honor to still be remembered and be a part of their lives.

Nanny Two:

"Special Needs Children: When you find someone who can connect with your child, do everything you can to keep them. I worked with a family for ten years on and off until their son was sent away to school. I would still work with him when he came home for breaks. His speech was very slow and babyish, and he also had epilepsy and balance issues. He had a small vocabulary and obsession with Rocky, the movie, and boxing. He was able to enjoy play times with the other kids in the neighborhood because he had a strong and committed advocate, me, his nanny, to help the other kids learn to enjoy and accept him."

Nanny Three:

A lot of being a nanny was good for me because I wasn't able to have children, and I wanted to experience that gift. I loved cuddling and making up stories and playing imaginary games.

I had a family who would set up their beanie babies all over the room. We would pretend that they were pets, and the other one would pick one out to purchase and pretend that I was the mommy. I loved them like they were my own. Doing their hair and spending quality time with them, for me, was always a special time.

During my interview with a family that had a four and 6-year-old, the 4-year-old climbed up in my lap during the interview. The family later called me to ask if I would work for them and told me their 4-year-old is a nervous child and doesn't go to anyone. We also used to paint together, and the kids got my inner artist activated! I went out one day and started painting; many of my works are throughout my home and others. I've since delighted friends with my works as gifts. I just think that letting the kids stay at home and being cared for in their home is the best way to take care of them when their parents are at work."

Chapter Eleven: From the Daycare Centers' Perspective

Daycare Center Interviews

Overwhelmingly, the daycare center directors who I interviewed always knew they would be working with children. One director said that when she was little, she would play imaginary games at home with imaginary children (her dolls) by teaching and playing board games with them. She later went on to earn a college degree in Communications with a minor in Early Childhood Development.

When interviewed, these women glowed with pride at their progression in their professional lives to director/owner of a daycare center. During our interview, there were multiple interruptions, which they handled with skill and charm. We were able to complete the questions, and I even got some (pleasantly) surprising additional information.

What has changed over the last 20 years in daycare centers?

Before we begin with the following interviews, I'd like to preface with this: since my kids were in a daycare center in the 90s (don't judge; I am still young at heart), the game has changed immensely. The education level now required for daycare center staff is one of the most significant game changes. Centers have gone from being glorified babysitters with a few fun activities to legitimate preschool early education programs on all levels, including infants starting at six weeks of age.

Daycare center teachers, on all levels, are getting their bachelor's and master's degrees. They are no longer just babysitting but truly educating your child in their classrooms. Parents are beginning to take notice as well. The daycare center is no longer just a safe haven but a learning haven for your child(ren). Every day planned age-appropriate activities are now required by most state jurisdictions.

I questioned how it was possible to plan for an infant and was pleasantly surprised at the answer. Even with infants, the staff work on core development, sitting, as well as fine and gross motor skills. Talking to the infants and giving them social interaction cues for social development is part of their planned activities. For example, when infants get positive facial expressions, they take on those characteristics. Let's face it: our children are awake in the daycare more than they are with us as parents, apart from weekends, of course. This time of alertness provides a rich opportunity for learning second languages and other mental and physical developmentally appropriate skills.

What Do Daycare Centers Want from You?

Of the daycare centers I interviewed, a common theme surrounding parental involvement emerged. The centers realize you are busy as a parent but would still like your participation in their programs. Today, there are provider/ parent conferences, much like school teacher/ parent conferences (oh, the joys of what you have to look forward to down the line!).

Daycare centers want you to be a part of the daycare center experience with your child(ren). The centers interviewed for this book encourage parents and family members to do an activity in their child(ren)'s classroom at least twice a year. This type of involvement exposes the other children to different teaching styles and cultures, for example, sharing your family traditions on a "show and tell" day. Having parental/family member involvement gives your child(ren) additional self-esteem and pride because their parent or family member took the time to participate in their daycare life. Another benefit is that you or your family members will be modeling leadership behaviors for your child to see you or family members in another capacity; this can go a long way in developing their leadership skills.

Some daycare centers will send homework home with your child(ren). They want to work with you as a team for your child's learning success. The homework can be as simple as counting how many doors and windows are in your home. If this isn't completed, the children can sometimes struggle when the other children share their homework results the next day. I like this idea because it prepares your child(ren) for the real world of academia and its pressure and rewards.

Believe it or not, daycare centers also want the lines of communication to be transparent and wide open, even when there is a complaint. They feel they can only improve when they receive feedback (both positive and negative) that can assist them with their program. Changes or modifications can be made based on your feedback. However, due to regulations and policies, there will also be times when the center cannot accommodate your requests, but they still want to have the opportunity to do so when they can.

Huge Mistakes We Make with Daycare Providers

Consistency!

Daycare centers ask kids to arrive by a certain time, usually between 7 am and 9 am, before their day starts. No longer are they the drop-and-go babysitter. Instead, many are now learning centers with daily plans and activities related to your child(ren). When you drop your child off at noon, for example, they miss all the activities from the morning. These activities can include circle time, small group activities, and outdoor activities, all of which give essential skills for interacting, taking turns, and building peer relationships.

When you consistently bring your child(ren) in tardy, they have limited time to play and are thrown into activities that have already been explained and started. They miss out on the morning activities and are then shortly put down for nap time. Typically, the afternoon has less going on due to nap time taking up a good chunk of time, so your child(ren) will miss out on key activities built for their success. Children need consistency in their lives, and a consistent schedule, whether at home or at daycare centers, is a great start.

Dress Your Child for Mess!

Creative play involves mess, like it or not. Whether it be finger painting, the sandbox, or making homemade playdough or slime, an apron can only do so much to protect your child's clothing. The whole point of these activities is to get the kids to learn by expanding their experiences and developing their skill sets. Some parents, however, don't want their children to get dirty or in the sandbox because the sand gets in their children's hair, and they have to wash it out. Psychology shows us that putting too many restraints on what your child(ren) can or can't do at the center limits their personal growth. Dress your kids in clothes that are okay for getting messy, and give the center a shower cap to put on them in the sandbox if that is indeed an issue for you.

For the Picky Parents!

Tolerance and understanding that your child(ren) is not the only one in the classroom being fed can go a long way in good relations with your daycare center providers, who may not be able to meet all of your demands. However, they will take note of what your child is eating, and they will try their best to accommodate your requests. And, of course, if your child has food allergies, this matter is much more urgent and non-negotiable.

Your Money Troubles

Many centers require deposits, ranging from one week to one month's tuition in advance. Sometimes, financial issues arise where families have difficulty making the upfront daycare center payment and the deposit. When this happens, some centers will work with you if you ask. Some daycare centers will put families on installment plans. What tends to happen, though, is that the families pay the deposit installments for a few payments with the weekly rate and then stop paying the deposit altogether. This default from some parents is not fair to the daycare center, which loses out on revenue. Families generally get back 100% of their deposit when they no longer use the daycare center. If they do not pay their deposit as agreed, it makes for an accounting nightmare and complications when your child is no longer using the center because you may still owe that money. And you will also lose out on receiving your two weeks' deposit back at the end of your child's stay.

Diapers!

Now, I am sure this will not be *your* experience, but...there are parents who let their children "sit in IT," if you know what I mean. Dropping your child off at daycare in a soaked diaper they wore all night is unfair to the child and their daycare provider. Additionally, the conditions for a nasty diaper rash, which can snowball out of control, are present when babies aren't correctly changed. If there was no way you could change your child before you left the house, or perhaps they had a bowel movement in transit to the daycare center, be sure to communicate this to your child's provider. This communication will save you both frustration and get your child immediate attention. Daycare centers also need you to supply enough diapers and wipes for your child, so they do not run out of them. Diaper changing stations are required by law to come with gloves, sanitation wipes, and sprays to prevent cross-contamination with other babies and toddlers.

Children with Special Needs

Many centers have special needs training. Before enrolling your child, they will give an Ages & Stages Questionnaire (ASQ); you can find an example on my website at WhosWatchingMyBaby.com. The ASQ looks at a child's developmental areas, such as fine/gross motor, cognitive, and social/emotional skills.

In addition, one of the centers interviewed uses *Healthy Beginnings*[7], developed by the Johns Hopkins University School of Education for the state of Maryland. This resource tells you where children should be developmentally at certain ages. For example, at four to eight months, a child should be able to express comfort and discomfort, enjoyment, and unhappiness. *Healthy Beginnings* focuses on personal and social, language, cognitive, and physical development. They also offer a great activity planner for various ages, from infants to toddlers, to promote early learning[8].

If a child is found to have special needs, centers will request them to take advantage of the resources offered by their county, such as an assigned therapist. The therapist then goes directly to the daycare center and provides assistance for free, as long as the parents are residents of the county. A team approach is created as the parents, daycare center, and therapist work together to assist the child in achieving the help they need. A progress meeting is set up with all three parties to ensure the child gets the support they need at the daycare center and home.

If an older child comes in with special needs, the daycare center may ask for an IFSP Individual Family Service Plan (for preschoolers); they will also try to follow this. One of the centers we spoke with has an inclusive program where they work to include children with special needs in their planned programs. They do this on a trial period to ensure the inclusion works positively for the child. They ensure the child fits the program; if they do not, they make other suitable recommendations and arrangements.

The center should ensure their staff are educated on a child's diagnosis to avoid any misinterpretation of that child's behavior. Teachers and Providers receive 12 hours, and their assistants receive 6 hours of continual annual training. That said, there are times when the daycare center's resources are not enough for special needs children, and they are unable to accommodate them.

When resources are exhausted in a daycare center, placing a child with special needs can be tough. While a lot of free state assistance is available, helping kids with special needs is difficult for both the center and the parents. Autistic children, depending on where they are on the spectrum, can be very challenging to place. Therefore, parents with special needs children may need to be hyper-vigilant and fight even harder for their child's rights to be accepted in a center that is qualified to have them.

Chapter Twelve: Useful Forms & Resources

Hiring childcare is a lot like running your own small business, so you'll need to be organized to ensure a positive outcome. I created the following tools based on best practices as well as my own need for order out of chaos. These forms have helped me to keep sane and not lose my mind during the process, regardless of your daycare solution type (center, in-home, au pairs, or nannies). For your convenience, you can find these forms and more in the Appendix or download them from my website at <website.com>:

1. In-Home Nanny Compare & Select Sheet
2. Daycare Center Compare & Select Sheet
3. Pre-Screening Questionnaire
4. In-Home Nanny Application
5. In-Home Interview Guide
6. Non-Residential Daycare Center Interview Guide
7. Residential Daycare Center Interview Guide
8. Reference Check Form
9. In-Home Work Agreement

Your State Government Regulations

Your state's government is a gold mine of information for childcare. If you Google [State + Childcare Regulations], your state's information will appear. Take your time going through the site to get acquainted with all that it has to offer. What you will find is information regarding:

- Regulations - Background checks
- Licensing Requirements for large and small daycares
- Credentialing
- Directories of in-home and regular daycare centers which are licensed.
- Subsidy forms if you need financial daycare assistance.
- Special needs assessments and services

Chapter Thirteen: Your Search Begins!

Okay…take a big breath and exhale. You have weighed the pros and cons of each daycare solution, and now you are ready to hire! On the face of it, this appears to be an easy task, and if you're lucky, it will be... but it's highly doubtful. It's often said that "the doctor and father are the first to know, and the childcare provider is the second;" there is a good reason for this saying, let me tell ya!

So, how do you know where to go and how to get the best solution for your choice? The following will provide you with a great starting point for your search. For each potential solution, I suggest you start looking while you are pregnant! It's not too soon because, as you will see, childcare is very fluid, and what is available today may or may not be available tomorrow. The early bird truly does get the worm in this case.

Word of mouth

Nothing beats someone else's experience. Especially if the person you are speaking with has used the center they are recommending or has hired the childcare provider you are considering in their own home. Let your friends, family, and coworkers know you are in the market; ask them if they know anyone who can help you.

Be specific when you are asking for a childcare recommendation. For example, if your social circles don't have personal experiences, ask if they know anyone who might know. I have found some of my best solutions this way, by getting a 2nd or 3rd hand referral from someone in my business and social circles. However, timing will always be a barrier with this type of search. I've often found the perfect person, only to discover they just took a job with another family. That said, don't get discouraged, and just keep asking!

Google and Yelp! Ratings & Reviews

When considering a nanny agency or daycare center, this is an excellent place to start your hunt, especially if you are new to an area and don't have a by-word-of-mouth support network you can go to for assistance. Google and Yelp! ratings are independent ratings; they cannot be manipulated as with some other sites. I like Google and Yelp! ratings better than Facebook because they are not "friends" of the business, but rather, Google and Yelp! users are leaving their comments independently. On Facebook, most of the time, it's like asking your besties to rate you, so this is why I don't recommend using them.

The lower ratings are the ones that I would start with on Google. Did the daycare center respond to the bad review? Did they offer the person to call them to talk or say they would be calling the person? Or does the daycare or agency have no clue they are even getting these ratings?

In an age of online reputation, you want to be sure you are dealing with a business that's taking care of business and reducing its liability for poor reviews by responding to them. Smart providers will acknowledge both negative and positive reviews promptly. They will take the time to offer a solution to the negative ones, which is a big clue to you that they take their business seriously.

Conversely, take heed if an agency or daycare center has all 5-star ratings. It is unlikely that this is very authentic.

The great part about Google is that people can express themselves, and rarely does anyone get all 5-star ratings unless asked to do so. To this point, some businesses will offer incentives for giving 5-star ratings, which is not a great practice. So, as with everything, use your judgment and common sense.

Nanny Agencies & Au Pair Agencies

Engaging a nanny agency will save you time but not money. Au Pair agencies are usually less than nanny agencies since you agree to house and treat the au pair as a family member. There will be an application, placement, and transportation fee, but it may be well worth it to have a well-screened candidate. Before selecting an agency, interviewing at least three of them would be advisable. My forms in the Appendix and on WhosWatchingMyBaby.com, under Resources, will navigate you through this process.

Most agencies won't turn you away, as could be the case with a daycare center at capacity because they typically keep a stockpile of screened caregivers. Another thing is that they do complete background checks (well, most of them; see Carla's Story). But again, you can refer to Google to see if the agency gets good reviews and what people say about them.

Quite often, if it's a big agency, you will have to go through the phone maze to get a live person. Remember to ask for an extension or direct number when you do get a human; I hated listening to all the prompts and never took the time to ask how I could get through more efficiently.

Many of these businesses meet with their nannies in person and do the background checks for you. You can expect to pay an agency application fee, usually from $99-

$199+, as well as a placement fee, which is typically 10-20+% of your nanny's salary (at $500/ week, that would be $2600 (10%) or $5200 (20%).

That said, a lot of these same nannies are on the nanny websites without the additional cost of a nanny agency. I interviewed quite a few nannies from the websites that were also part of a nanny agency. There are websites on which nannies put their profiles to find a family; they are much like dating sites with pictures, interests, and sometimes videos. By getting these nannies from these childcare sites instead of an agency, you can save a lot of dough and know they have gone through a background check. Still, just to be sure, consider doing your own background and reference checks if you go outside of an agency. Some of these background check companies are in the appendix and WhosWatchingMyBaby.com.

Online and Facebook Groups & Communities

There is a plethora of mommy groups online and on Facebook. A simple "mommy group" search will pull up endless options for you. Read what is already posted in the group so you are familiar with how they interact, and then figure out the best way to introduce yourself. Many of these groups are closed, and you must answer a few questions before requesting permission to be added. When you are added to a closed group, be sure to introduce yourself briefly and say something like:

"Hi there, thanks for the add. This is my cutie (if you are comfortable sharing a picture of your child(ren), include it in your post for more attention). We are looking for <insert your childcare choice> and would love any recommendations you might have. We live in <your

city/state> (if this is a national group, I would add your city/state; if it is hyper-local, you are good to go). Thanks!"

Daycare Centers

Depending on which daycare center you decide on, there may or may not be availability for your child(ren) when you need it. In some cases, people have paid centers earlier than when their child was due there just to keep that child's space and prevent another family from getting it. This reason alone is why you need to look at multiple centers and rank them in order of preference (see Daycare Center Compare-A-Gram sheet found in the Appendix and on WhosWatchingMyBaby.com).

During your interview, you'll want to look at least three daycare centers. Remember you are hiring them, so you must be 100% comfortable with the facility, attitude, and attention to you during the interview. You might also consider choosing a center close to your place of work and if they meet your requirements regarding hours and policies. A center close to your place of employment can be a big plus if you are a single parent. If you're a two-parent home, maybe you want them closer to your house so your partner, assuming you don't work close to each other, and you can take turns with pick up and drop off. My Daycare Center Interview Forms can be found in the appendix and WhosWatchingMyBaby.com to assist you in this process.

It can also be convenient to use the same daycare center as your friends and coworkers (*who you like*). This arrangement can save you in a crunch when you are sick or running late and need someone to cover for you. Additionally, you get to return the favor when they are in the same position. In your daycare center application forms, you'll need to put each other down with contact information to give each other pick-up and drop-off permissions when needed.

Other Options

You can also go "old school" and create flyers, newspaper ads, or make requests of your neighborhood/city online listservs, forums or social media. While these never worked out for me personally, they're all viable options and can work.

Chapter Fourteen: Pre-Screening Calls & Interview Questions

This chapter reviews each solution and what to be aware of to ensure you have the most positive experience possible. Each solution has its own characteristics, so you will want to take note of these when choosing what works best for you and your child(ren). In the Appendix, and under Resources on WhosWatchingMyBaby.com, I've also put together interview questions for each solution discussed and a Childcare Provider Application (for live-in and live-out nannies).

Pre-Screening Calls

Taking the time to interview is the key to a successful match for a quality childcare solution. Pre-screening is a process that should not be rushed or done out of desperation. Trust me on this! However, before you actually have an interview, you will want to set up a screening call. Screening calls can save you a ton of time and money.

My screening calls never went more than 5-10 minutes. My first observation was always how the person answered the phone versus how they spoke with me. Sometimes, they would answer abruptly and then start talking sweetly when they realized I was a prospective employer; take note of that. In the great words of Maya Angelou… "When someone shows you who they are, believe them!"

The purpose of your screening call is to make sure you don't waste your time traveling and conducting an interview. If the candidate isn't available to start when you need them or for the days/hours you need them, then meeting with them in person will be a complete waste of your time. For my complete Pre-Screening Form, see the Appendix or download it from WhosWatchingMyBaby.com under Resources with password "MyBabyResources!."

I always suggest having someone accompany you for in-person interviews for a second opinion and to watch your child(ren) if you bring them.

Daycare Center (DCC) - Non-Residential Interviews

Speak to the director and observe how they handle your questions. Did they give you a confident handshake and make you feel welcome, or did they barely touch your hand and leave you feeling like you were interrupting their day?

Quality DCCs should welcome your questions, realizing that you are taking their business seriously and aren't a "dump-and-go" parent. If they appear agitated, distracted, texting, or reading emails, they're not taking you seriously, and you should consider looking elsewhere. Remember, you are looking for someone to replace you when you are working, not picking out a place to have a birthday party. This decision is just too critical to get wrong, and your child's life will be in the hands of your chosen daycare center (DCC).

On the other hand, you should expect interruptions during your interview. The director is the go-to person, and a DCC is an active place. Staff will often need direction and guidance with specific administrative or child-related questions. These interruptions are also an excellent opportunity for you to observe staff and their interactions with their boss.

When writing this book, I was interrupted by a DCC while interviewing the director. The joy from her staff member, covered with grass stains on the back of her shirt and paint on the front, was evident. I asked the staff member how she got those stains, and she beamed about an engaging activity she and her kids did outside before nap time. The director apologized for the interruption, and I told her it was all alright. She happily answered the staff member's question and directed them on what to do; we then continued our interview.

Later, when I was touring around the center, I could see that it was definitely a happy and joyful environment. The staff were genuinely "present," loving what they were doing. They had no idea who I was because I was an observer with the director. Beyond the director/owner, you need to check out the staff, too. The best way to do this is to ask the director if you might "observe" the room where your child will be spending most of their time.

When deciding on a DCC, here are some things I looked at as a basis for comparison.

Considerations:

1. Hours of operation and how they fit with my schedule
2. Late pick-up policy and penalty
    a. Some will charge $1+/minute if you are late

   b. Others will give you some slack (I like those the best and never abused it)

3. Education and appearance of staff
4. Appearance of children
   a. Are the kids happy or stoic?
   b. How do they handle sick kids?
      i. Do they have a separate sick room from the rest of the center?'
      ii. Do they call parents to pick up their child if found to be sick?
      iii. How do they "define" sick kids and when you can or cannot bring your kid to them?
      iv. How do they "define" healthy kids after a sickness? (24 hours without fever?)
5. Is the center antiseptic looking? Does it look too neat, as in everything is in its place?
   a. Do they showcase the children's art?
   b. Is the art/decoration all store-bought with little arts & crafts activity from the children to be seen?
6. What is the selection/criteria process for their staff?
7. How long have they been open?
8. How long have different staff members been there?
   a. The last thing you want is for your child to play "musical chairs" with a DCC that

cannot retain its staff. Unhappy staff usually translates to unhappy kids.

9. Are shoe covers worn in their infant room?
10. What is the nap time sleeping arrangements?
    a. Cots, mats, or something else?
11. What is the "accident policy"?
    a. How do they report what happened, what was done, and how your child is doing?
12. Do they take the children off-site? If so, what is their procedure, and are you notified every time your child goes off-site (i.e., to the park, pool, or museum)?
13. What security measures do they have in place for emergencies?
    a. Is there a fire plan and place to go if they must evacuate?
    b. Is there a "shelter in place" plan for emergencies?
    c. Are there cameras where you can observe your child from your electronic devices?
    d. Is there a keypad for entrance at the door, or can anyone just walk in?
        i. If there is a keypad, how often do they change the code?
14. What is the physical appearance of the center?
    a. How is the paint on the outside and inside, as well as the landscaping?

   b. Do they take pride in the appearance of their business?

15. Are the toys clean and the equipment maintained?
    a. How and how often are toys and equipment sanitized?

16. Do they wear gloves for diaper changes?
    a. Is the diaper changing area well stocked with gloves and cleaning supplies?
    b. Are they sanitizing the changing station after each use, regardless of child?

17. How does the DCC manage someone other than you picking your child up to go home?
    a. There will be times when you are sick or unable to get your child. You need to plan for this ahead of time with a list of approved folks who can pick your child up; a good center will insist on this.

18. Do they use an app that you can download that will give them the same information as the My Day journals, such as the Bright Side App? The Bright Side App allows parents to get pictures and information about their child's eating, diaper changing, and napping directly on their cell phones!

19. Is there a hard copy or shared Google Drive journal on your child that documents diaper changes, food eaten (and not eaten), ounces of liquid ingested, and activities for infants and toddlers? I still have my daughters' "My Day" journals from her first DCC, and love to look at them occasionally.

Residential Daycare Centers

Licensed In-home Daycare Interviews

Licensed in-home daycare centers are run in homes and are like those in business settings. They're required to adhere to the state's regulations. For your convenience, I have provided a link to your state's childcare regulations in the Appendix and WhosWatchingMyBaby.com. When interviewing a licensed in-home daycare provider, it's best to call ahead and make an appointment. Not only is their center smaller than a non-residential daycare center, but it's also someone's private home.

Recently, many states have begun requiring lesson plans, record keeping, and various other regulations for residential daycare centers; this has some providers opting out as they are small, and the paperwork can be overwhelming. In my research, I spoke with a woman who said it was too much to keep up with while watching four small children, so she let her state license expire and continued as an unlicensed in-home daycare center.

In addition to the information for Non-Residential Daycare Centers, consider the following questions when comparing them to Residential Daycare Centers.

1. Who else lives in the home, and what is their interaction with the children in your care?
    a. While the state will do background checks on all residents in the house, if there are new residents since the state's investigation, you may want/need to do your own.
2. Where and how is food prepared for your child?

3. Is the center license visible and up to date? You can snap a quick picture with your cell phone to check the validity of the license online.
4. Are there clearly marked fire exits?
    a. If they are in a basement, how many exits are there; most guidelines require a minimum of two exits.
5. What is the adult-to-child ratio, and does it comply with your state's guidelines?
6. Is the space adequate for the number of children on-site?
7. Is the environment welcoming indoors and outdoors?
8. What are the required activities and lesson plans for the children?

Unlicensed In-home Daycare Interviews

Because this solution is not regulated, you must use your gut and a network of solid references, if available. My experience with one of these facilities was great and not so great with another, so it's really up to you to decide if this option is for you. You may have easier access to unlicensed centers compared to your licensed ones, but remember, they are not regulated and may not be following all of your state guidelines completely.

If you find an unlicensed in-home daycare you like, a background check on the provider and those living in the residence is highly suggested for your peace of mind. Also, speak with current parents about their experience, how long they've used this person, and their satisfaction level.

Additional considerations:

1. How many children are watched?
2. What are the ages of the children watched?
3. Who else, besides the provider, will be watching your child?
4. Who else lives in the home?

a. What are their ages, and what interaction will they have with your child?

5. What is the provider's backup plan when they are sick or take a vacation?

a. Some providers have friends who will jump in and take over for them; you want to meet them, too.

6. What is the changing station like?

a. Are there disposable gloves and sprays for sanitation?
b. Is there a safety strap for infants?
c. Is the surface washable?
d. Has it become a collection area with non-changing items?

7. Is the space adequate inside and outside for the number of kids they watch?

a. Is there a fence in the play area outside?

8. Is payment expected when the provider goes on vacation?
9. Is payment expected when you are sick or go on vacation?

Live-in & Live-out Nanny Interviews

First and foremost, no matter how tempting and time efficient, DO NOT interview in your home. Many of my interviews were conducted at fast food restaurants or active spaces like parks or indoor playgrounds. This is because you do not know if you will hire this person, and there is no need to expose your home to a stranger.

The questions and considerations for these positions are relatively the same, with the exception of establishing boundaries and space for the live-in nanny. Be sure you allot a minimum of an hour when setting up the appointment in the event you really like this person. I used to set up back-to-back interviews in the same place and use the time in between to rate and go over my interview applications and notes.

Additionally, bring your child(ren) to the interview, if possible, to see their reaction to this person. Especially if your child is verbal, which I *highly* recommend for in-home daycare, they can give you feedback on this person. One of my worst hires was a woman my daughter begged me not to hire; in hindsight, I should have listened to her. Once you get into the interview, bringing along someone who can entertain your child, like a spouse, significant other, family member, or friend, is a good idea. After small talk and introductions, begin each interview by giving your prospective nanny an application. You can use the one I created found in the appendix and under Resources on WhosWatchingMyBaby.com with password "MyBabyResources!."

Right off the bat, when you meet this person, take note of your gut reaction.

1. Are they pleasant or smiling? Do they have energy and seem genuinely interested in the prospect of in-home daycare?
2. Do they appear healthy, tired, or sickly?
3. Are their hygiene habits acceptable to you?

a. Hair, nails, scent (yes, scent, this person will live in your home or stay there for an extended period. Some cultures do not use deodorant, and if this is an issue for you, it is better to figure that out now than once you've hired them).

4. Do they interact with your child immediately, or do you have to force it via introduction?
5. How does your child respond to them?
6. Do they give you direct eye contact? While this is important, cultural norms vary drastically in this regard, so you'll need to go with your gut on this one if they are hiding something, shy, or if it is a cultural norm if you do not get direct eye contact.
7. What is their personality? Strict, Friendly, Shy, Bland, Bubbly? You know your child and how they respond to different personalities. Be sure this person exhibits traits you are looking for and that are compatible with your child's personality (and yours, too!).

If the interview goes well, and you do like this person, be careful NOT TO HIRE on the spot. It is crucial first to reflect, then go through the referral and background check (next chapter) before making an offer. Additionally, you are now essentially running a small business, and you want to have your offer in writing to go over with your nanny; this will ensure that you both understand what is being asked. It also allows them to ask you questions for clarification.

One big red flag is an applicant's unwillingness to fill out an application. It turns out that the woman I offered to fill out the application form for was illiterate, which could have been serious in an emergency or when giving medication to my children. By the way, she was the same applicant my daughter begged me not to hire...lesson learned.

In the Appendix and on WhosWatchingMyBaby.com, you'll find a Nanny Application, which can be filled out by anyone applying for your live-in or live-out position. These questions will allow both of you to figure out if you're a good match for each other, particularly when it comes to pets, smoking, and swimming, just to name a few. Be sure to read over the nanny's answers before you interview to become acquainted with them. Resist sending your interview questions out in advance. This avoids having the prospective nanny find someone to help them with their answers.

Placement Agencies: Nannies & Au Pairs

The purpose of an au pair agency is to work with you in narrowing down the au pairs you are interested in hiring. Keep in mind, though, there could be some language barriers, which you will need to adjust for if you like the person. Also, be sure to understand the replacement policy *before* you hire an au pair through an agency. Because some au pairs may overstate their qualifications to gain employment, they will say they can drive, swim, are CPR certified, etc. *(See the story of Carla).* In addition, it's important to note the following:

1. Do they have a current Visa, or will you have to purchase one for them?

1. If so, what type of Visa do they have, and when does it expire?

2. When are they available to start?

3. If they are already here, what happened with their original family placement? Can you speak with their former family?

4. Do they have a valid driving license? If so, go out and let them drive (just you) as part of your interview. Let them take you somewhere, like the post office, and see how they drive, use signals, and park.

Childcare Website Placement Agencies

Many nannies listed in private nanny placement agencies can also be found on childcare websites (i.e., Care.com, Nannies4hire, etc.). When interviewing, you want to ask prospective hires if they are listed with childcare placement agencies. If so, verify their agency listing; most agencies will have identifier numbers next to the pictures of their available nannies for hire. Ask for their number and verify the listing after your interview. Knowing they are listed with a professional agency also lets you know someone has met them face-to-face, and, more likely than not, a complete background check has been performed.

While I believe these sites are helpful, do your own due diligence and invest in your own background checks. I got one of my best nannies from one of these websites (see the story of Iris). That said, I also got an earful of information from her that completely floored me about how nannies conspire to help each other get hired on these websites.

Iris shared that many of the women on nanny sites act as each other's references. When I called her to interview with me, she was with her friend, who I literally had called within minutes of speaking with her for an additional interview. Both were references for each other, posing as moms and had other friends who did the same.

Despite your best efforts to screen thoroughly, you must be extra vigilant, particularly regarding childcare websites. These websites are electronic platforms with an expansive database of profiles. In most cases, they never meet their nannies face to face; they are much like a dating site for childcare.

If it's obvious you're speaking with a parent (like a kid calling "mommy!" in the background), go to your questions. Reference check questions can be found in the appendix or downloaded from WhosWatchingMyBaby.com. However, if there is an ounce of doubt, consider asking:

1. If you can meet them in person?
2. What do they do for a living, and where is their office?
3. How long is their commute/ what route do they find fastest?

These questions smoke out false references. Tying these questions into your reference check for your candidate in the event you are speaking to a real parent *will* stump the false reference of your intended hire. If they are stumped, swipe left and move on to another candidate.

Chapter Fifteen: The Background, Drug Screening & Reference Checks (In-home care only)

Congratulations! You're now excited about your choice and solution. It's time to do a reference check, and your form is ready to complete! However, the person on the other end of the line does not think your candidate is as great as you do. Believe them. Be wary of getting too emotionally invested in your candidate before you get a clean background and reference check. Then, and only then, should you start to get butterflies in your tummy.

Many companies offer background and drug screening checks; you cannot afford to leave your child in the wrong hands, especially in your home, where they are one-on-one with your childcare provider. You wouldn't want your perfect candidate watching your child if you found out they tested positive for illegal drugs or past criminal activities, would you? My intent is not to be dramatic but to assist you in making as fully informed a decision as you possibly can.

While background checks and drug screenings are additional expenses, they are well worth it. Also, by being open with your prospective candidate and letting them know there will be a background check and drug screening, you'll quickly weed out the ones who will test positive quickly (no pun intended, lol). Often, they will call you shortly after your interview to tell you they found another family or have a sick relative and must return to their country (oh yeah...I had that one too!). Don't be disappointed; be thankful you dodged a BIG bullet.

For a listing of background and drug screening companies, check out the Appendix or WhosWatchingMyBaby.com. Background checking is a critical step that you do not want to skip. Also, remember that you get what you pay for. Instant reports are just that, instant, and do not necessarily dive deep enough into a person's past on different databases. Ask lots of questions and read the fine print before deciding which screening company to use to check out your candidate.

Chapter Sixteen: The Hire

Nannies & Au Pairs

It's time to hire after your screenings and background checks have concluded with favorable results. Before hiring, though, I suggest scheduling a "just-to-be-sure interview," this time in your home and with your children. Invite your prospective nanny to your house and let them know you would like to have them there for 1-2 hours; you may offer to compensate them for their time if you'd like. The point here is to show the nanny around your home and introduce them to any pets, children, or other family members to see how you both feel and respond to one another. You also want to observe them with your children, so you will want to leave them alone with your child for a bit, but where you can still watch.

If all goes well within this time, you're almost ready to hire! I recommend having them play with your kids for at least an hour and thanking them for their time. Once the nanny has left, speak with your kids and other family members about their experience (if your kid is verbal, of course). Think about what you liked and what you thought may be an issue. If there are no major red flags, you have a final candidate! You're ready for lift-off! You've made a home run! Congratulations!

The number of final candidates you have will depend upon you and how many you want to run through the screening process. Remember, though, they are looking at other families besides yours, so you may want to have at least two final candidates in the event one gets hired before you're ready to hire them (yes, you guessed it, this has happened to me, too!).

Your next step is to select your final candidate and call them to offer the job. Then, you'll want to make a third meeting to review their "work agreement" found in the Appendix or on WhosWatchingMyBaby.com. While the process is laborious, it truly is worth it. After all, you are entrusting your most precious family member into the hands of someone you do not know. By taking these steps, you also show them you respect their time and profession and stack the cards in your favor for a long-term relationship with your nanny or au pair!

Electronic Devices/ Nanny Cams… Yes, or No?

With the evolution of technology comes the nanny cam and other electronic monitoring devices. I get asked a lot about my opinion on whether to use them or not to use them. I tend to go towards the "Golden Rule" when it comes to nanny cams: treat people the way you want to be treated. I wouldn't want to happen upon a camera watching me if I were taking care of someone's child. However, if I were told in advance that there were surveillance cameras in the home as part of a security system, I would be okay with that.

It doesn't pay to have a camera to catch your nanny in the act of abusing your child. You went through a rigorous screening process to hopefully alleviate any chance of that happening in the first place. We have all seen the horror recordings of nannies abusing children, which has struck fear into our hearts. I believe with proper communication (a common theme you'll repeatedly see from me), your childcare provider will be okay with you having "security cameras."

Especially if you make the cameras out to be a part of the security system in your home and not a spying device. It is better to be upfront than to offend a great nanny or au pair and have her decide you don't trust them and leave your employment.

Withholding Taxes... Yes, or No?

The United States Internal Revenue Service Department (IRS) has regulations regarding when to withhold taxes and when you don't have to withhold. The decision is up to you whether you want to withhold taxes or not. I have done both withholding and non-withholding, depending on the situation. There have been embarrassing cases of political officials who have not withheld taxes and were penalized. The decision is entirely up to you and your comfort level.

If you decide to withhold taxes, online calculators are available to help. Check out the appendix or WhosWatchingMyBaby.com for free childcare calculators. Knowing the ins and outs of your responsibilities as an employer is essential. With that responsibility comes filing quarterly taxes, employment tax, and correctly filing the appropriate forms. If you have an accountant, they can handle this for you as part of your regular tax preparation.

However, if you don't want to be bothered with all the forms and number crunching, that's okay. There are online companies that provide childcare tax withholding and payroll. They offer weekly paychecks, processing, quarterly tax filings, and year-end tax preparation (including W-2, W-3, and Schedule H), all for a moderate fee. Some of these companies can be found in the appendix and on WhosWatchingMyBaby.com.

Licensed Daycare Centers - Residential & Non-Residential

After you've had your tour of daycare centers and have narrowed them down to the one you like the most (or that you can get into in some cases), it's time to read the fine print. Before contracting with them, you will want to request a copy of their agreement so you can take your time reviewing it before signing. Because these contracts tend to be lengthy, reading them in your time and place of choice is a good idea. Once you get through it, you can address any items for clarity before signing with the center.

Be sure to pay attention to the deposit, the return of the deposit, their hours, and late fees if you are late picking up your child. You will also want to note if there are any additional fees or requirements, such as your participation (which I think is a great idea) or supplies, you will be responsible for bringing, such as lunch, diapers, extra clothes, etc., which are all reasonable.

Unlicensed Daycare Center

Rarely will there be any paperwork involved with an unlicensed daycare center. As long as you feel you have done your due diligence with screening the residence, you are ready to go (see Chapter 14 about pre-screening calls and Interview questions). Basically, you will agree with them on when your start date is and what your hours are going to be.

Because there is no paperwork, it's good to ask how they handle you being late if you are delayed. All your other questions should have been answered during your interview with them, such as their vacation time, when they get sick, and when you go on vacation. Don't leave anything to chance or surprise. Be sure to have all your questions answered and be ready to take your child(ren) if there is a vacancy on the agreed-upon start date.

Congratulations...You've made a home run!

Chapter Seventeen: The Inevitable - Backup Plan for

STORY: NEIGHBORLY LOVE!

A nasty snowstorm developed when I was in sales, and I couldn't get out of my house. To make matters worse, my nanny couldn't get to my home. My boss told me that if I didn't make it into the office, he would not honor the $10,000 sale I had just made from my kitchen table, worth $2,000 to me in commissions.

I will always remember my neighbors helping me dig out of my driveway. They were kind and watched my children while I made my way downtown. When I arrived at the office, less than pleasant, my boss called me into his office and told me, "Your childcare problems are of no importance to me." His opinion was very easy for a man with a stay-at-home wife and three kids to say; I was horrified. I will forever be grateful to my amazing neighbors for their acts of kindness. In their collective wisdom, my neighbors also told me to get another job. I took that advice to heart and left that company and sexist boss the following spring!

I got a great new job (and a supercharged snow blower) and loved them both! Inevitably, there was a snow day. Panicked, I called my new boss to say I couldn't leave my neighborhood but would work diligently from home. She said to enjoy my kids, go play in the snow, and have a fun snow day. Beyond elated does not even begin to describe how I felt. I put the snowsuits on my girls and let them and the dogs have at it in the front yard. I proceeded to snow blow not only my driveway but also the driveways of the three other neighbors who had helped dig me out the previous winter.

Your Backup Plan

All is well in your dominion until the bottom drops out due to an unforeseen circumstance. Your nanny calls in sick, you are ill and cannot get your child to the daycare center, the weather is terrible, and your daycare center is closed, but your office is open and expecting you. Today, it's not enough to have a backup plan; you need a backup to your backup plan to ensure your sanity. I literally had four layers of help in the wings in the event the first three weren't available. My network of family, friends, coworkers, sitters, and drop-in daycare centers was, and needed to be, extensive.

My best advice here is to create a list of who could watch your child(ren) if your daycare is unavailable for a myriad of reasons. Start with your neighbors, if you know and trust them, and go down the line to family, friends, and colleagues. One of my best nannies was a beautician at JC Penney's who overheard my plight on finding good daycare. She said she would work her hours around mine and was with us for three years. To this day, we are best of friends and share milestones and family events together (see story about Mariza).

Additionally, you can start shopping around and get your child registered or accepted on a "drop-in" basis at residential and non-residential daycare centers. The online websites also offer sitters who are available as well. According to Sitter City, Inc., 2,000 sitters join their site every day[9], and they have a category of "Occasional" for backup care. In this case, it would be great to go through the interview process and have these sitters on standby in the event you need them.

KinderCare Education at Work[10] is a large national daycare chain offering a variety of backup options to companies for a fee. If you work for one of these companies, you get an online portal that gives you 10% off on daycare, backup care, and priority enrollment. As with all daycare centers, you want to check and interview them yourself. However, it's good to know there are some real viable solutions available to you when the unexpected arises.

Finally, you'll also need a backup plan if your solution is a daycare center with those per-minute fees if you are late. For me as a single mom, I registered a bunch of my close friends who I trusted to have permission to pick up my kids. They would go to the daycare center for me, take the kids to their home, or put my kids in their car until I got there to pick them up. I also had a password with my kids that they would ask anyone picking them up for, this worked out great and thank goodness they were never picked up by an unauthorized person.

One time, when I was running late, I asked my long-time and trusted dear friend Ellsworth to pick up my kids from the daycare center. We agreed that he would wait with them in his car until I arrived. I will never forget the shock and awe on his face as my two 3- and 5-year-olds happily swirled around his SUV, excited that Ellsworth had come to pick them up! I could barely say thank you, or open the door to retrieve them, because I was laughing so hard.

Chapter Eighteen: The End - When Change Happens

According to the National Conference of State Legislatures[11], all states are "at-will" [for employment] except for Montana. This means that you can terminate the employment of a nanny without cause. However, given everything you went through to place this person in your home, you will most likely have a reason, which we will discuss in a moment.

Changing your childcare solution can happen for many reasons. You may end up getting laid off and unable to afford the current childcare you once could. Maybe your daycare provider is closing, if it's a daycare center, or your nanny announces she must go back to her country to care for a sick relative (note: this last one is not always truthful, but if they don't want to be with you, let them go). Regardless of the reason, it's going to have an impact on you and your child(ren).

Speak with Your Children

Remember, your child is the one who spends more time with this person, or center, than with you. If verbal, explain to them straightforwardly that there has been a change. With that change, they are safe because they will always be with you. Furthermore, you are working on, or have found, a new childcare solution for them.

If it is a positive termination, like your nanny graduated college and is now going into the work world, work with your child (if verbal) to have a special celebration. You can celebrate with food, crafts, a party, or whatever works best for you and your budget. This lets the nanny know they are loved, valued, and teaches your child that not all change is bad. This celebration of their daycare provider allows them to have a healthy, positive transition and closure experience with someone they have spent much time with and cared for.

For me, when I knew someone wasn't working out, I whipped out my interview sheets and started the hiring process before I fired the current nanny. I would let the current nanny go on a Friday and start a new one the following Monday. Over that weekend, I would make a soft introduction to the new nanny. Because my kids were verbal at the time, I elected not to include them in replacement nanny interviews. The last thing I needed was for them to tell the current nanny she was being fired!

How to Fire with Dignity and Grace

Let's face it: nobody wants to deliver bad news. Letting a nanny or au pair go is very different than letting go of a daycare center. Because your nanny/au pair is in your home, there becomes more of a familial relationship. That relationship, though, can sometimes be taken advantage of, leading your childcare provider to be "too comfortable" and not doing what they agreed to do when they were hired. Either way, termination is no fun and can confuse your child and upset your childcare provider.

In-Home Provider Termination

Because you will have your work agreement (see Appendix or WhosWatchingMyBaby.com) and your monthly check-in meetings, a termination for failing to do the job should not be a surprise. Particularly if your child is fond of this provider, it is imperative to give them every chance. One way to keep on track or alert your provider to an issue is to follow up your monthly meetings with minutes or a light-toned email or text confirming what was discussed and agreed upon during your meeting.

That said, there are deal breakers such as consistent tardiness (which in turn makes you late for work), breaking any family rules such as no smoking, overnight guests, drinking or drugging while caring for your child(ren), or whatever you deem to be non-negotiable. When calling it quits, you'll want to try to get a replacement in the wings or at least tap into your backups to cover you until a suitable replacement can be found (see Chapter 17: Backups for Your Backups).

Whether you want to give severance pay or not is up to you. Unless someone was utterly incompetent, I always paid two weeks of severance. My thought was that the payment would lighten the blow of them losing employment and assist them in finding work elsewhere.

If your termination is because you can no longer afford the provider, as was when I was laid off, it is an entirely different conversation. Assure them that you will give them the best reference for any new opportunities they pursue. You may wish to provide them with more than two weeks of severance since this termination had nothing to do with their performance.

Licensed Daycare Center Termination (Residential & Non-Residential)

When you join a licensed daycare, you receive a contract outlining their policies and procedures. Terminating your agreement with them should be clearly outlined in the contract. Be sure to know what is required and the consequences thereof before signing the contract. When you no longer utilize the facility, you must provide them with what is necessary to terminate your agreement.

If you're moving or school is starting for your child(ren), and you no longer need the center but had a great time there, you may want to do something special. Suggestions include bringing staff treats, gifts, thank-you notes, or cupcakes. While not in daycare, when my daughter left elementary school, we took her favorite teacher out for sushi as a thank-you. These ideas go a long way in showing appreciation and teaching your child the value of thanking and appreciating those who have been kind to them.

Unlicensed Residential Daycare Termination

Because there are no real rules and regulations with unlicensed residential daycare centers, it is best to give as much advance notice as possible. Giving advance notice allows the provider to look for someone to fill your child's spot. The more sophisticated unlicensed residential centers may take an initial deposit and keep it as your last one or two weeks. Others will simply accept your verbal notification.

Again, if you are parting on a good note, it's nice to show appreciation to the staff and teach your child the value of a thank you. Having your child craft something like a picture frame with their picture in it is always nice. One of the unlicensed centers I interviewed beamed when she showed me framed photos and calendars of her past children's art who are now either grown or in school. These folks work hard (well, at least the good ones!), so I always liked to show appreciation.

Start Over and Keep Positive

The words "Rinse...Lather...Repeat" seem to come to mind here. You've already completed finding the right childcare solution at least once, and now it is time to do it again. If you need a refresher, you can use this book as a resource and make it your own by writing down your thoughts and plan of action in the margins or on the blank pages at the end of this book. The good news, though, is that there will always be a childcare solution available. It is up to you to determine which one meets your family's best needs, budget, and schedule.

Having a positive attitude and injecting A LOT of humor got me through some of the most insane situations; honestly, I could not have made this stuff up. My friends still laugh with me today about how many different childcare solutions I went through. My children (see Chapter 20: *From a Child's Point of View*) will tell you that we went through childcare providers like water. The good news is that my girls came out just fine, and we are still good friends with the majority of the women who cared for them.

I admit I did a lot wrong when selecting my childcare solutions. I wish I had had guidance when I was searching for childcare, which is what gave me the idea for this book.

I figured I didn't go through all of this for no reason, and it has allowed me to give parents a head start on the process and hopefully help them avoid many of the mistakes I made.

Chapter Nineteen: How COVID-19 Has Changed Childcare

The COVID-19 pandemic has significantly impacted the childcare industry, including preschool and infant care. Below, I have gathered some of the effects of COVID-19 on preschool childcare and infant care. As you read through the rest of the book, keep in mind the new landscape that infant and preschool childcare is now dealing with. Understanding the effect of COVID-19 and how it has changed our infant and preschool care will allow you to make the best decision for your child's care when you are working.

1. **Changes in Operating Hours:** Due to the pandemic, many preschools and infant care centers have had to adjust their operating hours. Some centers have reduced their hours, while others have implemented split shifts to simultaneously reduce the number of children in the center.

2. **Decreased Enrollment:** With so many parents working from home or losing their jobs due to the pandemic, the demand for childcare services has fallen. This decrease has led to many infant care centers and preschools experiencing a decline in enrollment, which has had a negative impact on their finances.

3. **Increased Health and Safety Protocols**: The pandemic has resulted in improved health and safety protocols in daycare centers and preschools. These include daily temperature checks, frequent

hand washing, wearing masks, and social distancing. Centers have also increased their cleaning and disinfecting procedures for toys and high-touch areas to reduce the risk of transmission.

4. **Staffing Challenges**: The pandemic has led to staffing challenges for many daycare centers and preschools. With increased health and safety protocols and decreased enrollment, some centers have had to lay off staff or reduce their hours. This has led to increased workloads for remaining staff, which can lead to burnout and decreased quality of care.

5. **Financial Hardships:** Many daycare centers and preschools have experienced financial hardships due to the pandemic. With decreased enrollment and increased operating costs, many centers have struggled to stay afloat. Some centers have had to close permanently, which has had a negative impact on the families and children who relied on them for care.

6. **Reduced access to care:** One of the most significant effects of COVID-19 on daycare centers and preschools has been the reduced access to care. Many childcare centers and schools were forced to close or reduce their capacity to comply with social distancing requirements, leaving parents in a lurch and scrambling to find alternative care arrangements. This disruption in childcare has significantly impacted families and the workforce, particularly parents who have had to take on additional responsibilities at home.

7. **Increased demand for care:** On the other hand, some parents have faced increased demands for

childcare due to changes in their work arrangements. For instance, parents who previously worked from home have had to return to their workplaces and now require full-time care for their children. This has led to a surge in demand for childcare services in some areas.

8. **Changes in regulations:** The pandemic has also resulted in changes in rules governing infant care centers and preschool childcare. Centers have had to adapt their operations to comply with new health and safety guidelines, which have increased their operational costs. Centers have also had to make significant changes to their policies and procedures to limit the spread of the virus, such as requiring face masks for staff and children and implementing frequent handwashing and sanitizing.

9. **Mental health impacts:** The pandemic has also had significant mental health impacts on both children and their caregivers. Children may experience anxiety and stress due to the disruption of their routines and social interactions. On the other hand, caregivers have had to manage increased workloads, added health and safety concerns, and the emotional toll of caring for children during a pandemic.

10. **Increased technology use:** The pandemic has also led to an increase in the use of technology in preschool childcare and infant care. Many centers have had to adopt virtual learning platforms to continue providing education and support to families. Additionally, parents have had to rely on technology to communicate with caregivers and monitor their children's development.

So, as you can see, the COVID-19 pandemic has significantly impacted infant care and preschool childcare both during and after COVID-19. From changes in operating hours to increased health and safety protocols, the pandemic has presented many challenges for centers and families alike. It is essential for the childcare industry to continue to adapt and innovate to provide quality care to children during these uncertain times.

Sources:

1. [2] National Women's Law Center. (2020). Childcare in crisis: Understanding the effects of the COVID-19 pandemic on childcare programs and families. Retrieved from **https://nwlc.org/resources/child-care-in-crisis-understanding-the-effects-of-the-covid-19-pandemic-on-child-care-programs-and-families/**
2. Centers for Disease Control and Prevention. (2021). Guidance for childcare programs that remain open. Retrieved from **https://www.cdc.gov/coronavirus/2019-ncov/community/schools-childcare/guidance-for-childcare.html**
3. National Association for the Education of Young Children. (2021). COVID-19's impact on childcare. Retrieved from **https://www.naeyc.org/resources/topics/covid-19's-impact-child-care**
4. American Rescue Plan Act of 2021, H.R. 1319, 117th Cong. (2021). Retrieved from **https://www.congress.gov/bill/117th-congress/house-bill/1319**

Chapter Twenty: From a Child's Point of View

It occurred to me while writing this book that all angles were covered except that of the end user, that being the child who receives the care. Following are the perspectives from both of my beloved girls (young ladies now) and whom you have gotten to know through our stories in the previous pages. I personally invite you to consider the rich perspective each of my now adult daughters brings to the table as you select the childcare that works best for your family. As you will see, there is no perfect solution and they all have costs, some lifelong, as well as benefits.

Emily (First born)

"Growing up, my world revolved around routine and nannies. They were the ones who took me to school, held my scraped knees, and saw me the most. While my friends rattled off stories of soccer practice and school plays with their moms, mine were filled with trips to the park, baking blueberry muffins, and Nannies patiently trying to teach me Spanish. There was a sense of calm, an unwavering presence in our home that I attribute to them.

Looking back, I can pinpoint the benefits of having Nannies at the helm. My days were structured yet open-ended, filled with exploration and learning tailored to my interests. Nannies knew every nook and cranny of the home, transforming trips to the grocery store into scavenger hunts and rainy afternoons into fort-building expeditions. With them, I discovered a love for musical movies, different cultures and religions, as well as new communities. Nannies challenged me intellectually, nurturing my curiosity and fueling my thirst for knowledge. My favorite ones always made me laugh and I missed them greatly after their time came.

Though it was a tapestry woven with love and laughter, there were, of course, threads of longing. There were times when a lovely park trip, however captivating, couldn't fill the void of my mother's absence. Moments when watching other kids rush into their mothers' arms after school sparked a pang of jealousy. The "why" questions, once met with Nannies gentle explanations, began to carry a new weight, an unspoken resentment towards a woman whose career kept her away. It was often a bittersweet ache, a realization that the security and love Nannies so generously offered couldn't erase the yearning for the mother who was mostly just out of reach.

While the benefits & memories of my nanny-centric upbringing are undeniable, the tapestry of my childhood remains one woven with both golden threads of new connections and the occasional knot of bittersweet longing.

In my adult life, I realize that my mom's sacrifice was well worth it for my sister and me to be afforded a life that so supported our dreams.

I feel like mothers, single ones especially, often carry the burden of having to do it all and my mom was no exception to this rule.

I am grateful for the care labor of both my mom and my nannies, as well as their undying love and support."

Maya (Da Baby!)

"Growing up with babysitters, nannies and au pairs was *interesting*. I'll also add that I hated daycare, and that environment was extremely stressful for me. I was a very introverted child, and extremely attached to my mom. I saw the women coming into our home as a placeholder for my mom, often fulfilling my physical needs but rarely the emotional needs of my sister and I. Some of my nannies were incredibly patient and loving, even after my snarky and uninterested interviews with them. I've remained friends with a handful of these women, and truly view them as family. Others were cold, unqualified or simply not good at the job in any way, which left me with a great distrust for future sitters. Some exited their jobs without saying a word, others I would hear being fired from the room next door.

Now don't get me wrong, I knew my single mom needed help and we all benefited from the privilege of being able to afford extra care around the house. I enjoyed having rides to school instead of taking the bus, not having to worry about making dinner and even having someone to take me to social events during the school week. It was convenient and allowed me to truly be a kid without parentified responsibilities. But no matter how much I liked (or didn't like) the current nanny, I always wished that my mom was spending more time with us. I remember asking to be homeschooled or to have endless nights sleeping in my mom's bed just to spend extra time with her.

Now as an adult, I can recognize the codependency I felt with my mom. Her leaving while it was still dark in the morning and coming home after dinner for much of my young childhood created an abandonment wound that I'm still healing today. My upbringing and childcare have also heavily influenced how I think about *my* future, and if I even want to have kids or not. I saw the ways my mom worked so hard to be there and present when she could, but inevitably still missed out on our everyday lives and even some milestones. She chose to keep up her successful career and work life to provide us a comfortable lifestyle and opportunities. When we were together on the weekends, holidays, or vacations, life felt like a movie. We always had so much fun. Then in high school when she left corporate America and became her own boss, we got rid of our babysitters and had to pull back on just about everything. I started taking the bus home from school, began helping with cooking dinners more and even grocery shopping. We pulled back on eating out, vacations and spending all together - but I was able to have more time with my mom. I enjoyed this time greatly, but as a teenager my schedule was constantly full. I didn't have that same childhood desire to be with my mom 24/7 at that point. I had hours of homework, extracurriculars and began focusing on applying to college.

The world looked a lot different in the 90's and early 2000's than it does today. I look at the hard decisions my mom had to make and wonder if I could do the same. Could I have a family and prioritize my career? What sacrifices would I have to make if I ever became a mother? Is there a world where I can de-center "motherhood" all together and find fulfillment in other areas of life? In this economy and with how challenging the world is right now- I often wonder how it will all pan out for me. I learned so much from my mother, her resilience and leadership are unmatched. No parent is perfect, no childhood is either, but I'm ultimately very thankful for the way I was brought up."

When each daughter sent me her write up that you just read, I literally had tears in my eyes. I didn't realize how much my childcare choices for them impacted their precious little lives and even to some extent, their lives today. I am so grateful that we are still close knit and have an incredibly loving relationship.

I will never forget though how much it hurt both of us that we had to be apart so that I could provide for them and make a life for us as a single mom. I resented the hell out of bosses I had that wouldn't allow me to attend field trips or special events with my kids.

My own mom, who has since passed, provided a haven of love and support to me and my girls as well. I wouldn't be who I am without the great Lois Bell (Nana) and how much she taught me (the good, the bad and the ugly too!) about being a mom."

Chapter Twenty-One: The Conclusion (well at least mine!)

There's no place like HOME! Aka...MOM & DAD!

So now you've seen what I've learned from my daughter's childcare journey from 4 months old through high school. It was one of my life's most stressful and challenging times, trying to keep my work, home, and daycare lives all in order. If I had to do it all over again, I would probably do my best to figure out how I could stay at home for at least part of the week to be with my baby. According to Pew Research, it's beneficial to younger and older kids [12] for a parent to stay at home. Staying home was never a choice for me due to my personal and financial situation of being a single mom.

However, if there is any way you can extend your maternity/paternity leave and take advantage of the Family and Medical Leave Act of 1993 (FMLA), I would suggest you do. FMLA leave can be extended up to one year. To be eligible, you must have been working for 12 months at your place of employment, comprising 50 or more employees within 75 miles of your office or worksite. This leave is unpaid, but if you can bank your vacation, personal, and sick leave, you can live off those savings. For complete information, you can download the U.S. Department of Labor's FMLA brochure at Tinyurl.com/FMLABrochure.[13].

Thank you so much for your time in reading this collaboration of my experiences and those who contributed. I hope you find this as entertaining as you did a valuable resource for yourself. I'd love your feedback and welcome you to contact me at Christina@WhosWatchingMyBaby.com with your experiences and/or any suggestions. The website WhosWatchingMyBaby.com is also a great place to retrieve all my forms and items discussed previously and even buy a copy for an expecting friend (smile).

It has been years since I had this idea as a book, and I finally found the time to get it out of me. Over the years, many of my friends have told me this book is a great idea and consistently asked me when I would write and publish it. My answer was always the same, "I am just looking for some time to do it; it is so much." Then I realized that God didn't put me through all that drama for nothing, and I owe it to you, the reader, to get it done!

I had no clue why I kept putting off writing this book. When I would search the internet, I couldn't find a resource such as what I put together here, so of course, that made me feel even more guilty for not doing this sooner! So, I quickly concluded that my insane childcare experiences weren't for nothing. They were to teach me, broaden my outlook and knowledge on EVERY type of childcare possible, and most importantly, to help YOU!

Be Blessed,

Christina Eaglin

PS. All the forms, questionnaires and guides can be downloaded from my website at

WhosWatchingMyBaby.com under Resources with the password “MyBabyResources!.”

PPS. Let me know your thoughts on this book and if you found it valuable. Was there something more I could have included? While I tried to include everything, I would have wanted when I was looking for childcare, I am open to additional requests for future publishing and the website.

About the Author

When Christina Eaglin had her first child, she was a Senior Account Executive at NBC4 television in Washington, D.C. Her infant daughter commuted with her husband and attended a federal government daycare center. This solution worked well for their new family; she would pack the diaper bags, and her husband would transport their daughter to the daycare center.

When she had her second daughter, she successfully hired away one of the federal government daycare employees to become a nanny in her home. However, when her girls were just six months and two years old, she got a divorce and had to change childcare solutions. From then on, and through her kids completing high school, a series of nannies lived in and lived out of their home. She went through over 13 childcare solutions including: nannies, shared nannies, au pairs, licensed daycare centers, in-home daycare centers, both licensed and unlicensed. Because of her career, the in-home childcare solution worked best for her and her girls. As her daughters got older, they renamed the position from "Nanny" to "House Manager!"

During this time, she also changed jobs to become a Director of Integrated Marketing at the CBS Affiliate in Washington, DC. From there, she became the Director of Interactive Marketing for Children's National Medical Center. Confronted with an unexpected layoff, she came home to recreate herself and started her own business.

Today, Christina and her girls are still in touch and friends with many of the incredible women who assisted them by providing childcare. She is President of MVP Agency, LLC, (Marketing, Video Production, and Public Relations).

Christina took everything she learned from the corporate world and created a unique boutique agency solution for her clients. In her most recent chapter of life, she has taken all she learned from numerous childcare solutions to help parents all across the world. This book was written over the course of twenty years, during her first attempt at publishing, COVID-19 stopped her efforts dead in their tracks.

By her friends and family, Christina is known as the go-to mom for childcare solutions. Her energy and passion for children and their safety come from her first job as an assistant babysitter at the age of 10! She was also a live-in nanny for two families over six years.

She is available for speaking engagements, book clubs, and public appearances via the following email: info@WhosWatchingMyBaby.com. Christina Eaglin lives in Colesville, Maryland, where she raised her two daughters, who are now successful young businesswomen.

Resources

The following resources are downloadable at WhosWatchingMyBaby.com or by scanning this QR code and using the password, "MyChildcareResources!" (case sensitive).

Daycare Centers:

Daycare Compare-a-gram Spreadsheet

Non-Residential Daycare Center Interview Guide

Residential Daycare Center Interview Guide

In-Home Nannies or Au Pairs:

In-Home Nanny Compare & Select Sheet

In-Home Au Pair Compare & Select Sheet

In-Home Nanny Pre-Screening Questionnaire

Nanny Application

Nanny Interview Questions

Reference Check Form

Work Agreement

Stay-at-Home Parent Online Courses

Childcare Payroll Companies with Free Nanny Calculators

State Regulations
http://www.childcareaware.org/resources/map/

Background Check Companies

ASQ Sample: Go to:
http://tinyurl.com/ASQQuestionnaire (be sure to put in 2 "Q's")

---

[1] https://socialwelfare.library.vcu.edu/programs/child-care-the-american-history/ (accessed 6/26/19)

[3] Childcare Resource Handbook - OPM: https://tinyurl.com/OPMRHB (accessed 9/7/18)

[4] *The U.S. Department of Justice. Office of Sex Offender Sentencing, Monitoring, Apprehending, Registering, and Tracking (SMART):* https://tinyurl.com/verifysexoffenders (accessed August 9, 2018)

[5] *Metro Parent for Southeast Michigan. Stay-at-Home Moms More Depressed, Angry and Sad, Study Says:* https://tinyurl.com/SadSAHM (accessed September 4. 2018)

[6] Scarlata Kate. "Is Your Child on the BEIGE DIET," Baystate parent: https://tinyurl.com/Beigediet (accessed 8/8/18)

[7] Johns Hopkins School of Education. "Healthy Beginnings," Maryland State Department of Education: http://olms.cte.jhu.edu/olms2/healthybeginnings (accessed 9/25/18)

[8] Johns Hopkins School of Education. "Healthy Beginnings Activity Planner," Maryland State Department of Education: http://pfs.cte.jhu.edu/pf/pfs/healthy-beginnings (accessed 9/25/18)

[9] https://www.sittercity.com (accessed August 8, 2018)

[10] http://www.kindercare.com/employer-sponsored-child-care (accessed August 8, 2018)

[11] http://www.ncsl.org/research/labor-and-employment/at-will-employment-overview.aspx (accessed August 8, 2018)

[12] Pew Research https://www.verywellfamily.com/research-stay-at-home-moms-4047911 (accessed August 6, 2018)

[13] FMLA Brochure https://www.dol.gov/whd/fmla/employeeguide.pdf (accessed August 6, 2018)

APPENDIX

Daycare Compare-a-gram Spreadsheet

Daycare Center Comparagram Spreadsheet

Date	Name	Location	Request Visit Yes or No	Visited & Interviewd Yes or No	Positives	Negatives	Selecet Yes or No

Non-Residential Daycare Interview Guide

Many of these questions can be answered online from the center's website; however, it's still essential to have a face-to-face interview with a prospective daycare center. Be sure to read Chapters 2 and 3 on the pros and cons of licensed and unlicensed daycare centers. These questions are in no particular order. Feel free to rearrange and add some more of your own.

1. What ages do you serve?
2. How do you keep the children separated? (If there is a significant difference in ages, i.e., infant and 4-year-olds)
3. What programs do you have? (full-time, part-time, pre-school, before/after school care, etc.)

4. Is there a waiting list for your center at this time?
5. What are your center's priorities? (Education? Safety? Socialization?)
6. How many children are currently enrolled, and what is your capacity?
    a. How many square feet does your center have? *According to the U.S. government, children should have a minimum of 35 square feet of a usable play area inside and 75 square feet of outside useable play area space.*
7. Does your staff have CPR training?
8. What is your policy if I am late in picking up my child?
9. What is your policy on sick kids?
10. What is your policy on potty training and kids not potty trained?
11. What is a typical day like for a child my age?
12. What is your policy if I take a vacation, or my child doesn't come in?
13. What days are you closed? (Holidays? Local school closing? Professional days?)
14. How are children disciplined in your center's care?
15. What, if any, participation do you expect from parents?
16. Where, if any, places do you take the children offsite, and at what ages?

Daycare Center Interview Guide (Residential)

Many of these questions can be answered online from the center's website; however, having a face-to-face interview with a prospective daycare center is still important. Be sure to read Chapter 3 on the pros and cons of In-Home Daycare Centers. These questions are in no particular order. Feel free to rearrange and add some more of your own.

1. What ages do you serve?
2. How do you separate the children (if there are significant age differences)?
3. What programs do you have? (full-time, part-time, pre-school, before/after school care, etc.)
4. Do you have a waiting list?
5. What are your priorities for the children in your care? (Education? Safety? Socialization?)
6. How many children are currently here, and how many will you take?
7. How many square feet does your center have? *According to the U.S. government, children should have a minimum of 35 square feet of a usable play area inside and 75 square feet of outside useable play area space.*
8. Do you and your staff (if any) have CPR training?
9. What is your policy if I am late in picking up my child?
10. What is your policy on sick kids?
11. What is your policy on potty training and kids not potty trained?

12. What is a typical day like for a child my age?
13. What is your policy if I take a vacation, or my child doesn't come in?
14. What days are you closed? (Holidays? Local school closing? Professional days?)
15. How are children disciplined in your center's care?
16. Where, if any, places do you take the children offsite, and at what ages?

In-home Nanny Pre-Screening Questionnaire

Applicant______________________________________

Phone: ______________________________________

Email: ______________________________________

Screening Grade: ______________________________

In-Person Interview (circle one): YES NO

Initial feelings from the call:

____

____

____

NOTE: Before you jump into the questions, exchange pleasantries and thank them for their interest in your position. You can gauge their energy level and interest from their voice during this time. Then, be sure to review what you are looking for BEFORE you ask them questions (see script below); you don't want to go through this process to find out they hate dogs, and you have three dogs!

This prescreening process is a numbers game, and the more potential nannies you speak with over the phone, the better your odds are at narrowing them down to about 3-5 in-person interviews. Finally, you will narrow them down to 2-3 and then select your nanny. Speak with a smile and be engaging; remember the Golden Rule: would you want to work for someone with zero energy and personality? As with all of my forms, the following is just a suggestion based on my experience; feel free to modify them and make them your own.

Your Script:

Can I review the requirements of this position with you before I ask you some questions?

I have (ages/sex of your child/ren) and am looking for (full-time/part-time) in-home care. The job requires that (list out all that you are looking for here so there are no surprises):

a. Days, hours, live-in or out
b. Transportation of kids
c. Light housework
d. Cooking
e. Laundry
f. CPR or First Aid (you can let them know if they don't have this, you can provide training)
g. Swimming

Does this sound like a job you would be interested in doing?

- Now, this is where it can get tricky. For instance, a nanny told me her car was in the shop but would be repaired soon (spoiler alert: It never appeared after I hired her!).
- If they say "Yes, but…" See if the but is negotiable to you or if you need them to have everything you request.
- If they are good with it all, then it's time to jump into the questions:

Great, I'd like to ask you some questions now.

Your Questions (lines are intentionally wide spaced for you to write in the answers to your questions)

1. What experience do you have with caring for children, and at what ages?
2. Why do you like to care for children?
3. Where do you live?
    - You will want to ensure they live relatively close, so you don't have to depend on the unpredictability of traffic delaying them. If they need a lift, you can sometimes get to them or bring them to you quickly.
4. Do you have a car (if you want them to transport your kids and you won't be providing a vehicle for them)?
5. What is the highest level of education you completed, and at what school?
    - If someone mentions college, then ask, "What was your major in school?"
    - Sometimes, they are students and will work their class schedule around yours.
6. Are you currently employed, and if so, where and what are your responsibilities? How will accepting this position impact your current employment?
7. When would you be available to start with our family if I were to hire you?
8. If you meet the prerequisites for this position, we will follow up our conversation today with an in-depth face-to-face interview. Lastly, if it is determined you meet all the qualifications and characteristics for this position, and you and I are a good fit, then the last step in the process is a background check and drug screening.

- If there is no resistance to this statement, and you like what you hear thus far, proceed with the face-to-face interview.

Face-To-Face Interview…You Like Them!

Time to schedule that in-person interview! I always found it best to pick a date and block of time when I could meet with several potential nannies outside of my home, of course. See my suggestions in Chapter 14: *Pre-Screening Calls & Interview Questions* to get the most out of your interview.

You Don't Think They Will Be for You:

If you are not satisfied with their answers, thank them for their time and let them know that you are still looking and will get back in touch with them. Be sure to get their contact information or a way to communicate with them. Let them know you are not interested if you decide not to hire them.

Again, the Golden Rule applies here as you would probably want to know if you were or were not in the running for a position. You do not have to get into why you aren't picking them; just let them know, as a courtesy, that they are not being considered at this time. You can send them a friendly email like this:

Dear <applicant name>,

Thank you for speaking with me on the phone (day and time) regarding my childcare needs. As promised, I am updating you on our search for a childcare provider. We have gone with another candidate; however, I wish you the best in your search for a childcare position. If anything changes, I will keep your information. ***(I would only put this last sentence in if you "think" you may have to circle back if things don't work out with your current pool of candidates)***

Sincerely,

You □

In-Home Nanny Compare & Select

Date	Name	Age	Rating [A, B, or C] *Only hire A-rated Nannies B only if you have no A's	Phone	Phone Interview Yes or No	Book In-Person Interview Yes or No	In-Person Interview Yes or No	Hire Yes or No

Sheet

Nanny Application

Applicant Information

Full Name: ______________________________Date __________

Address:____

____

Phone: ____

Email: ____

Date Available: ____

Social Security Number: ____________________________________

Emergency Contact: _______________________________________

Relationship: ____

Phone Numbers: ____

Education Information

High School Attended: ____________________________________
Diploma? (circle one) Yes No

Graduation date: ____

College Attended: ______________________________
Diploma? (circle one) Yes No

Graduation date: ______________________________

Degree: ______________________________

Other : ____________________________ Completed?
(circle one) Yes No

Reference Information (3)

1. Name: ___________Relationship: ______________

Years known: _________

Phone:___________________________

Relationship:____________________

Years known: ________ Phone: _________________

Past 5 Years of Child Care History

Please list the positions you have had in the last five years related to your caring for children. You may include babysitting, summer camps, daycare centers, etc.

Job:____

Supervisor:__________________________________

Title: _______________________________________

Phone:______________________________________

Responsibilities: _______________________________

____

Dates: From ________________ to __________ (Month and Year)

Days and hours per week: __________________________

The reason it ended: ______________________________

Do you drive? Yes No (circle one)

Applicant Information

License State & Number ____________________________

Have you had CPR Training? Yes No (circle one)

If yes, when did you last update your training?

____

Do you swim? Yes No (circle one)

Are you comfortable with kids in water? Yes No (circle one)

Have you ever been convicted of a felony? Yes No (circle one)

Have you completed first-aid training? Yes No (circle one)

If yes, when did you last update your training?

____

Any health issues that could affect your ability to work?
Yes No (circle one)

If yes, please explain: ______________________________

Do you smoke? Yes No (circle one)

Do you have allergies to pets? Yes No (circle one)

Are you willing to assist in caring for a pet? Yes No

(circle one)

Please Rate yourself on a scale of 1-5, with 5 being the highest:

___ Patience

___ Maturity

___ Capable of making friends

___ Capable of being a self-starter

___ Capable of relating to adults

___ Ability to relate to children

___ Temper control

___ Sense of humor

___ Honesty

___ Tidiness

What do you enjoy most about working with children?

What do you enjoy the least about working with children?

How do you handle discipline and setting limits with children?

Other Information

I affirm that I have never been judged by any court to be the parent of a child in need of protection, nor have I ever been convicted of neglect or abuse or the subject of a claim of neglect or abuse.

I affirm that, if hired, I will not take any alcohol, narcotics, or any other substance that may impair my ability to do my job.

I affirm that all the information I have given on the application is accurate to the best of my knowledge.

Signature

Date

Nanny Interview Questionnaire

1. What is it about taking care of children that you enjoy most?

2. What do children like the most about you?

3. When did you last care for a child?

a. How long did you stay with the family?

b. Why did that childcare position end?

4. Have you had any other kinds of jobs besides childcare? If so, what were they?

a. What did you like best about each experience?

b. What did you least like about each experience?

Note: When you do references, be sure to cross-check the answers they give here for the length of employment and reasons for leaving their positions.

5. How long do you feel you would be willing to stay in this position?

6. Do you have any health issues that we need to be aware of, such as medical conditions that would prevent you from doing this job?

7. Do you drive?

a. Do you have a car and a current license?

b. What type of license do you have?

c. Would you be willing to drive my child(ren) in your car as long as I paid for your gas?

8. Do you cook?

a. What are some of your favorite dishes to cook for children (if they cook)

9. Do you live on your own? (for live-out positions)

a. How would you rate your ability to keep a house neat from 1-5, with 5 being extremely neat and clean?

10. On the rare occasion that we/I have to work late or go on a business trip over a weekend, could you arrange to take care of my child(ren)?

11. Tell me about a time you had to handle an emergency.

a. What happened, and how did you respond?

12. How did you grow up as a child?

13. Tell me about your family when you were growing up: what did they like, what did they not like, and how did they get along?

14. What is your relationship with your family today?

a. Would your family be in support of you taking this position?

15. Do you have friends who are nannies?

16. What do you do for fun?

17. What do you do to wind down and relax?

18. What would you say are your strong points that you like most about yourself?

19. Tell me what areas you would like to improve yourself.

20. What are your favorite television shows?

21. Describe yourself in three words.

INFANT QUESTIONS [0-12 Months]

1. How do you handle a crying baby?
    a. If the baby doesn't stop crying, what do you do?
2. Do you think babies should be held when they are fed?
3. How would you comfort a baby who was clearly tired and needing a nap?
4. What would you do to entertain a baby?
5. What do you feel is most important about keeping an infant safe?
6. (If you have a pet) Do you have any issues with (dogs, cats, mice, hamsters, etc.)?
    a. Would you be willing to assist in the care of our pet?

TODDLER QUESTIONS [1-3 Years]

1. How do you handle a child who doesn't listen to you and is stubborn?
2. Have you ever potty trained a child?
    a. If so, how did you do it? What was most important?
3. What do you like to do with toddlers for fun and entertainment?
4. If my child refuses to eat, how would you respond?
5. Do you have any favorite nursery rhymes or songs you like to share with children?
6. Do you like to read to children?
    a. What are some of your favorite books?
7. (If you have a pet) Do you have any issues with (dogs, cats, mice, hamsters, etc.)?
    a. Would you be willing to assist in the care of our pet?

PRESCHOOL QUESTIONS [4-5 Years]

1. What amount of time do you feel is appropriate for a child to watch television?
2. How much time would you allow for a child to play with electronic games?
3. What would you do for fun with my child(ren) inside the home?
4. What would you do for fun with my child(ren) outside?
5. How would you handle a situation in which my child misbehaved?
6. (If you have a pet) Do you have any issues with (dogs, cats, mice, hamsters, etc.)?
    a. Would you be willing to assist in the care of our pet?

SCHOOL-AGE CHILDREN [5-18]

1. Are you okay with other children coming to the house to play with my child(ren)?
2. How would you deal with my children if they were fighting each other?
3. What are your thoughts on helping out with homework?
4. Should my children need to get to school and activities, would you be okay with driving them around?
5. (If you have a pet) Do you have any issues with (dogs, cats, mice, hamsters, etc.)?
    a. Would you be willing to assist in the care of our pet?

Reference Check Form

Applicant Date

Reference Name

Reference Relationship

Phone Best time to call?

QUESTIONS:

1. How long have you known <name>?
2. What is your relationship with <name>?
3. Are they currently taking care of your child?
    a. (if yes) How long have they been caring for your child?
    b. (if no) Have they cared for your child in the past?
        i. When would you say they started, and for how long did they work for you?
4. Was <name's> work consistent or intermittent with you?
5. How many hours a week did they work for you?
    a. What was their schedule?
6. What were the ages of your kids when <name> cared for them? Do you have boys or girls?
7. What were <name's> responsibilities when they worked for you?
8. Why did (or will) they end their working relationship with you?

9. Do you know of any medical or mental illness that would prohibit <name> from doing their job?
10. Do you know of any drug or alcohol abuse that they may have?
11. What is the work ethic of <name>?
    a. Did they start work on time?
    b. Did they frequently get sick?
12. Tell me about their reliability, maturity, and ability to handle stressful situations like emergencies.
13. How would you characterize their ability to engage children?
    a. Are they fun to play with?
    b. Are they creative?
    c. Do they have a natural love of children?
14. How would you characterize their ability to discipline children when necessary?
    a. Are they strict?
    b. Do they give consequences?
    c. Do they consult with you about your preference for discipline when you are not around?
15. What are their strengths?
16. What are their weaknesses?
17. Tell me how they are with taking your direction.
    a. Do they listen to you?
    b. Do they feel comfortable offering other ideas?

   c. How do they handle constructive criticism from you?

18. Would you hire them again if you needed childcare?

    a. If not, why not?

19. Thank you so much for your information. Is there anything else you would like to say or add to the questions I have asked today?

Work Agreement

<NAME> WORK AGREEMENT

<Name> agrees to the following:

Hours:

* House Management/Childcare services will be provided Monday through Friday from

[Start time] to [End time] on a [live-out / live-in basis]

Salary and benefits:

First six months: $XXX/week plus $XX for gas - $XXX/week

Second six months $XXX/week plus $XX for gas - $XXX/week

Second year $XXX/week plus $XX gas - $XXX/week

a. Salary will be paid by [cash/check / direct deposit] every Friday for days worked.
b. Holidays are given as [unpaid/paid] days off unless you are needed and agree to work.
c. Health insurance will be covered by <name>.
d. One week of paid vacation will be given after six months of employment, and two weeks of paid vacation will be given after twelve months. Vacation weeks are to be mutually agreed upon and align with our family vacations as much as possible.

Job Responsibilities:

- Food preparation for [breakfast/lunch/dinner and snacks]. Feeding and cleaning up the kitchen after meals with the exception of dinner (especially pots, pans, the stove, coffee pot, and dishes in the sink)
- Transportation to activities for the children (money for any parking or recreational activities will always be paid in advance)
- Within mutually agreed upon and defined limits, <name> will care for visiting friend's children at no extra charge unless previously arranged.
- Keeping the house straightened and uncluttered.
- Directing children to put away misplaced items.
- Sweeping the kitchen and bathroom floors as needed.
- Daily emptying of all household trash cans (bedrooms, bathrooms, and kitchen).
- Checking on and replacing items such as toilet paper, Kleenex, paper towels, lotion or soap when they have run out.
- Keeping upstairs bathrooms and guest bathroom clean (keeping all surfaces clean on a daily basis, Spray cleaner under each sink)
- [Children's/Family] laundry to be washed, folded, and put away (supervision of children in putting their own laundry away).
- Shopping for groceries or other errands such as the cleaners or post office.

- Daily supervision of the feeding and care of the family pet
- Being responsible for the grocery list for food and household items. Adding items to the Costco list that the household needs as well.
- Keeping the house locked and secured at all times.

Other:

We are always available to discuss any concerns or ideas you may have. Please know that you can call either of us at any time. My cell (XXX) XXX-XXX.

b. Congratulations on your new job, and welcome to our home!

<Name> / Date

<You> / Date

Stay-at-Home Parent Online Courses

Because I Said So, Baby

Because I Said So, Mama

Thoughtful Parent

Childcare Payroll Companies with Free Nanny Calculators

HomePay: Best Overall

NannyChex: Best for payroll taxes

OnPay: Best for small budgets

QuickBooks Payroll: Best for QuickBooks users

Paychex Flex: Best mobile app

SurePayroll: Best for auto payroll

Justworks: Best for professional employer organization (PEO) services

Care.com HomePay

Poppins Payroll

Simple Nanny Payroll

Sure Payroll

The Nanny Tax Company

Background Check Companies

ClearChecks

Enannysource

Nanny Verify

ShareAble

Legal Disclaimer: These companies are not associated with our book, and we do not make any guarantees. As with any financial decision, seek legal help if you have questions.

YOUR THOUGHTS AND NOTES

What are my non-negotiables?

What is my ideal childcare solution?

Who would be the ideal person to take care of my child(ren) when I cannot?

Who can I rely on as my back up(s)

www.ingramcontent.com/pod-product-compliance
Lightning Source LLC
La Vergne TN
LVHW051836080426
835512LV00018B/2901
* 9 7 9 8 2 1 8 3 7 8 7 1 4 *